RETURNING TO LEARNING?

Studying as an adult: tips, traps and triumphs

CAROLINE BREM

ALLEN & UNWIN

First published in 1996

Allen & Unwin Pty Ltd
9 Atchison Street, St Leonards, NSW 2065 Australia

Phone: (61 2) 9901 4088
Fax: (61 2) 9906 2218
E-mail: 100252.103@compuserve.com

National Library of Australia
Cataloguing-in-Publication entry:

Brem, Caroline.
  Returning to learning?: studying as an adult: tips,
  traps and triumphs.

  ISBN 1 86448 071 8.

  1. Adult education. 2. Study skills. I. Title.

374.1302812

Set in Futura and 11/13.5 pt Garamond by DOCUPRO, Sydney
Printed by Australian Print Group, Maryborough, Victoria

10 9 8 7 6 5 4 3 2 1

This book is dedicated to John, Cheryl, Daniel and Natalie who gave me the space, time, freedom and encouragement to write it. I know I'll never be able to repay them.

Do not say 'When I have leisure I shall study'. You may never have any leisure.

Hillel

Contents

Foreword

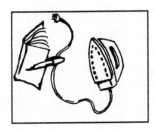

Even the longest journey starts with a single step.

Chinese proverb

THE BEST WAY TO START ANY JOURNEY IS TO IDENTIFY THAT FIRST STEP, and it isn't always as obvious as you'd think. When you travel, buying the ticket is not the first step. When you want to study, enrolment is not the first step either. Both events begin with a dream.

We all have dreams, it's what we do with them that makes each one of us different from the other. If you dismiss them as nothing more than fantasies they'll never come true, but with a little imagination, a lot of determination and some faith in yourself you can make any—or all—your dreams come true.

My dream was to get a university degree but I hated school with a passion and left as soon as I could convince my parents that I should. I did this by the simple expedient of not doing any work in the year I turned 15. My father decided that it was a clear case of the horse and the water, and helped me to find a job. Fortunately he didn't think I

ix

was stupid or lazy, just stubborn and wilful. So I worked, travelled, got married, had kids—in short did all the things a female member of the middle classes in the 1950s and '60s was expected to do. Then, when I hit that magical 40 I started wondering what it was all about.

Now my dream has changed: I'd like a PhD even if my kids say it's only because I want people to call me Doctor. But more than that, I want to help others to improve their lives. I know that study isn't the only way to do that, and it isn't even always the best way, but it is the only way I have at present.

So, take your dreams out of that box in the bottom of the cupboard where they've been gathering dust for years, shake them out, have a look at them, think about them, don't show them to anyone else until you've brought them up to date, but don't throw any of them out until you're sure you no longer want them. Only you can make your dreams come true!

So you've decided to think really seriously about studying something. As a mature-age student you have a lot of options: from hobbies you can learn from a friend or neighbour to that PhD you always knew you could get.

By mature-age students I don't mean any particular age range, but rather anyone who, having left school, went to work (or tried to find work and couldn't) and then decided to seek further education of some kind or another. You may have done your HSC 2–3 years ago or, perhaps like a great many of my students, you left school at about 15 or 16 and have been working for somewhere between 10 and 25 years. Just thinking about learning scares you. The thought of competing with all those bright young students makes you blush. What will happen if I say something stupid? Will they laugh at me? Will they even talk to me? How will I remember all that new stuff? Am I too old to learn? These are just some of the questions that will be answered—or nipped in the bud—in the rest of this book.

Make sure you are really interested in the subject. There is absolutely no point in enrolling in the beginners' French class if what you really want to learn about is computer programming. On the other hand, you may want to enrol in a subject you already know something about. This could make all the difference to your final outcome because it puts you on that success spiral. So, don't be afraid: have a go.

Introduction

I DECIDED TO WRITE THIS BOOK FOR TWO reasons, but I can't say which of them came first or which is more important. One is that after teaching adults for many years I realised that their needs and expectations were very different to those of school students. The other reason is that, although there are many books on study skills available, most of them seem to be written for 16–18-year-olds doing the last two years of high school.

Most important of all, though, is the fact that I was a mature-age student myself. I left school at 15 for two reasons: I hated it and I wanted to travel. Until I got married at 25 I did travel and I worked in a whole range of jobs that included office work, waitressing, dish-washing and fruit-picking. None of these gave me any mental stimulation, but there was always a pay packet at the end of the work.

Then I discovered that some of the skills my grand-mother taught me were not being taught to others by their grandmothers. I began to teach friends to knit clothes for their new babies. I taught crochet and tatting and patchwork and embroidery. Then I began teaching the language in which my grandmother had taught me—German.

And then, one day my husband found in a Sydney newspaper an advertisement that read 'Are you teaching without qualifications?' or something like that. Sydney CAE was offering a new course, an Associate Diploma in Adult Education. To qualify for entry you had to be working as a teacher of some kind.

I was 40 years old; it was 25 years since I'd been to school and I didn't think I'd really learnt much in the interim. The thought of going back was both frightening and exciting. Everybody was going to be much cleverer, more experienced, more successful and more confident than me. But I did think it would be fun to try. That was in 1981. By the time you read this book I hope to have finished an MA after having gone on from the Associate Diploma to a BEd and a BA. Now that's either masochism or madness, I'm not sure which.

The way I think you should use this book is as follows: first read it straight through. Use a pencil—highlighter pens always seem to soak through to the other side of the page—and as you come across points at which you say 'aha' either underline them or put a mark or comment in the margin. Don't be afraid to mark the book—it's yours! Making notes and comments will help you find things again later and also help you to 'process' the information. Like most of the learning you'll do, you'll remember the information you stopped to think about. After all, you're not a parrot, or a photocopier.

Once you've read all the way through, put the book aside, but in a spot where you'll see it often. When you feel depressed or disheartened, pick it up and look through some of the chapters that seem to relate to the cause of your current problem. I hope I've made it positive and encouraging enough to help you over the bumpy patches along the way.

At the end of the long summer holidays, read it again while you're deciding whether to re-enrol in another year's study. But beware: you may end up like me—an education junkie.

PART 1

The student in you

1

In the beginning . . .

'I could tell you my adventures—beginning from this morning,' said Alice a little timidly; 'but it's no use going back to yesterday, because I was a different person then.'

Lewis Carroll

WELL, NOT COMPLETELY DIFFERENT, BUT CERTAINLY NOT EXACTLY THE same. And today you bought this book which means that you intend studying something and you're a bit nervous about what it'll be like.

I'll tell you: it's like jumping in at the deep end and I'm throwing you a lifebelt.

Early negatives

If, like many mature-age students, you left school early, perhaps you did so because you were told you weren't smart enough to go on. Or perhaps you grew up in an environment where education was not highly valued. Somehow your attitude has changed or you wouldn't be reading this book.

Who told you that you weren't smart enough to study? Who told you that you were? Whose opinion do you value more highly? Which of these people knew you better? Who do you want to believe?

Perhaps your attitude is only just beginning to change and the title of this book seemed to point in the right direction. I'll do my best to help you change but I must warn you: only you can change yourself. I don't have any control over you. And to bring about any changes in your attitudes, your health, your behaviour, your job—anywhere—you must first want to change.

You can change your attitude

How much and how quickly you change will depend entirely on your motivation, on how much you want to change. Once you make a commitment—to yourself, not to anyone else—you have to decide how you will bring the changes about.

Because attitudes are shaped by beliefs, and affect our behaviour, we have to change our beliefs to alter our attitudes and behaviour. When we believe something, we act as if it is true. Our actions—or behaviour—then reinforce our beliefs which, in turn, reinforce our attitudes.

It's important to realise that our attitudes, which have been shaped by past experiences, are the blueprint for our future. They govern so much of our behaviour that our future becomes quite predictable. In other words, if you always do what you've always done, you'll always get what you've always got. Remember, your attitudes are not something you were born with, like the colour of your eyes. Throughout our lives our attitudes are changed by experiences, influences and circumstances.

To see how this works, think of something you dislike intensely. What made you hate it? When did you begin to feel this way about it? Make some notes: see if you can discover what triggered the dislike, then decide if it is really worth maintaining.

Bad attitudes

Bad attitudes or beliefs—about yourself and your ability to study—limit you. They are the things you think you can't do. Let's say you'd like to learn to ski but you have never done it. Do you tell yourself 'I can't ski'? If so, how did you come to that conclusion?

Telling yourself you can't is limiting. If you think you can't, you probably won't even try. On the other hand, you can always give yourself permission to have a go.

Now, because we are concerned about study skills here, stop for a few minutes and make a list of the limits you have placed on your ability to study. Your list may contain such things as:

- I can't write essays.
- I can't remember information.
- I'm too dumb.
- I'm too old to learn anything new.

Put this list aside for a while and read on; we'll look at it again a little later in this chapter.

Good attitudes

Good attitudes give you permission to succeed. They let you find out what could be true and how capable you are. Remember, it's amazing what you can achieve when you don't know what you can't do. It is all too easy to know what you can't do. I can't cook. But how do I know I can't? I've tried, and having tried, I was unhappy with the result. This is legitimate. If I really wanted to be able to cook well, I would keep trying until I did succeed. The fact that I gave up indicates that this skill was not important to me.

So, developing a positive attitude is about reassessing our goals; about deciding how badly we want something. If you want something badly enough you will find ways to

5

overcome the obstacles. And bad attitudes, bad self-image and low self-esteem are just obstacles that can be overcome if you want to study successfully.

Believe and make-believe

> 'I can't believe that!' said Alice.
>
> 'Can't you?' the Queen said in a pitying tone. 'Try again: draw a long breath, and shut your eyes.'
>
> Alice laughed. 'There's no use trying,' she said. 'One can't believe impossible things.'
>
> 'I dare say you haven't had much practice,' said the Queen. 'When I was your age, I always did it for half an hour a day. Why, sometimes I've believed as many as six impossible things before breakfast.'
>
> *Alice Through the Looking Glass*
> Lewis Carroll

There is a German proverb which says that if you convince yourself of something then it will be true. So, when we believe something we act *as if* it is true, and then it can become true. When you were young most of your attitudes and beliefs about yourself were formed this way. A parent or other significant adult may have said something like 'Susie's such a tomboy' in an admiring voice. Susie picked up on the admiration, decided that this was something good and kept trying more and more daring acts. On the other hand, if someone had said 'Tommy's not much good at football' Tommy might have seen this as a reason for not getting any better at the game, especially if he didn't want to prove that person wrong.

Einstein believed that the universe is a friendly place. Do you believe that you live in a friendly place? If you don't, then try to imagine how this belief could change your attitude to life.

Go back to your list now and choose one of the statements about yourself that you would like to change, and write down some of the things that led you to believe it. What attitude or belief would you have to change to reverse this statement? If it's the statement that says: 'I'm too dumb', ask yourself how you know this.

Did someone tell you? If yes, when? Was that person important to you? Do you believe everything they tell you?

Imagination is powerful

The most powerful way to use your mind is to imagine yourself in a situation or position you would like to be in. If you are about to begin a course of study, try imagining yourself walking up to the stage to collect your Diploma. How well you can 'see' the picture in your mind will affect the final outcome. If there is a little voice inside your head saying, 'Ha, ha, you're just kidding yourself', then you are very likely to find a perfectly 'legitimate' reason to drop the course before the end. On the other hand, if you can get rid of that little demon, and really 'see' yourself shaking hands with the Head of School and collecting that diploma, there is an exceptionally good chance that you will overcome any obstacles and succeed.

All this, of course, takes practice. You need to begin by using some relaxation techniques. This exercise takes only about 5–6 minutes each time you practise it: find a quiet spot where you can sit down comfortably, then relax and concentrate on your breathing. When it becomes slow and regular, stop thinking about it and start to build up the picture of the graduation ceremony. Try to imagine as much detail as possible. Perhaps, in preparation for this exercise, you could check out the hall where graduation ceremonies are held if you have not been to someone else's graduation. The aim is to make your mental image as realistic as possible. Practise this once or twice a day for a week or so. By that time you should be able to call the picture to mind fairly quickly. The next step is to call it to mind in other circumstances—that is, without having to relax or breathe deeply.

Now, any time you have a problem and you start asking yourself why on earth you are doing this course, imagine your graduation 'picture'. You'll find that it will come to mind very easily if you did the initial practice exercises thoroughly. Having mastered this method you'll find that you can use it for all sorts of personal goals. More important, you will find it very useful for improving your memory.

Remember: not every suggestion in this book will work for everyone, but you'll never know which ones work for you until you give them a fair trial. And a fair trial is not one half-hearted attempt but an honest attempt two or three times. So, think of a short-term goal you would like to achieve. It may be to learn how to deal with the bugs on your roses—think how beautiful the flowers will look when you succeed!—or to enrol for that course—think about the achievement when you finish it!

First imagine the goal, then imagine the first step you must take to reach it. In Chapter 9 we look at a variety of ways to improve your ability to learn and remember things, but the method just described forms the basis for most of the others. It is also a good way to relieve stress and ease tension without drugs or other medication. See Chapter 6 for more about this.

Try role-playing

Another way to change an attitude is to role-play the attitude and behaviour you want to adopt. At first this may seem strange and uncomfortable, but with some practice this can also work well. Let's assume that you are afraid of going into the classroom because you think people will laugh at you. First, make a list of exactly what you think they will find amusing. One student, Peter, thought people would make fun of him because he was much older than he

8

thought the other students would be. He also thought that the other (younger) students would 'know' much more than he would.

Peter was persuaded to visit one of the student counsellors, Alan, at the college he was planning to attend. Although Alan assured him that other students in the class would be at least as old as he was, Peter was not convinced. So Alan did some role-playing with him. Alan suggested that he would be 'Peter' and come into the room, where Peter would be one of a bunch of younger students. When Alan-as-Peter came into the room he smiled at Peter-as-student, said 'Good morning' and sat down. When Peter-as-student didn't say anything further Alan-as-Alan asked whether this was realistic. Peter had to admit that it was highly likely that the students wouldn't take much notice of him. Alan then suggested that Peter might like to try out some other situations that were worrying him. For instance, they practised what to do when the teacher asked a question Peter couldn't answer. If the question was directed to the class in general there was nothing wrong with remaining silent and waiting for someone else to speak. On the other hand, if Peter was asked directly and he didn't know the answer, he could simply say so. But this took quite a bit of practice because Peter thought he would lose face if he couldn't give the answer.

Role-playing 'difficult' scenes is really just a more practical way of imagining the changes you want to make. The drawback of role-playing is that it works better with a partner to play the 'other' role. Unless you have acting skills and a good imagination, it is difficult to play both sides yourself.

Find a friend or fellow student to practise difficult situations with. When you talk with other students you may find that some of their problems differ from yours, but I'm willing to bet that some of them will also be very similar to yours. Sometimes just talking about them to other students is a help.

Other people's attitudes

Other people's attitudes also come in two flavours: they are compatible with ours, or else we find them strange in some way. The attitudes we find strange don't fit in with our own: they may be only slightly different, or the exact opposite. In either case, we may find it hard to understand how they think and behave.

As I said earlier in this chapter, the only person you can change is you. I now want to add a bit to this statement: your behaviour can be changed (temporarily) by someone else's behaviour—and remember, behaviour is really just an outward manifestation of attitude. So, if someone behaves in a certain way because of an attitude they hold, and that person has a position of influence, then the people around them tend to act in a similar way. If you don't have the same attitude but you behave as someone else wants you to behave, you will feel uncomfortable, either at the time or later.

To withstand someone else's attitude and behaviour we need a strong sense of our own identity. This comes back to having a high level of self-esteem. When you value yourself and you believe that your attitudes and standards of behaviour are acceptable it becomes easier to withstand pressure from others.

This matter of self-esteem becomes even more important when, as mature-age students, we expose ourselves to the influences of teachers and other students. There is no point in giving the teacher all the credibility. If you think the teacher's attitude doesn't match yours, don't be afraid to ask questions, make statements and generally clarify matters. In Chapter 3 we discuss the difference between assertive and aggressive behaviour and how to express your needs and feelings. Here I would just say that you can ask questions and make statements in a non-threatening, assertive manner without antagonising the teacher or the other students. In fact, you may find that some students will be grateful to you for doing so.

A good book for learning assertiveness skills, even though it is now about 20 years old, is called *When I say no, I feel guilty* by Manuel J. Smith. It contains lots of practice dialogues that help you to deal with a wide variety of situations in various ways.

Conclusion

You may think your attitudes are fixed, so the first thing you have to learn is that you can really change them if you want. Then, choose small areas of your behaviour which you believe need changing: anything that seems to limit your ability to reach your goals. It's easier to replace one kind of behaviour with another (better) kind than to try to eliminate something altogether. So think carefully about the behaviour you want to change and what alternatives you could try. Read Chapter 4 to learn about goal-setting and find out how to chart the way to your goal, then reassess your attitudes. In that chapter we look at the method of dealing with small, manageable chunks, and the reason for behaviour modification then becomes clearer.

2

What type of student are you?

GETTING TO KNOW WHAT TYPE OF STUDENT you are will help you in two ways: you'll get the most out of your preferred way of working and you'll increase your range of practice. Learning is a process that should bring a reward of some kind. This reward may be simply your satisfaction at achieving your goal; or it may be the diploma or a job you really want. By learning how you learn best you will be able to choose the activities that help and avoid those that don't. More than that, though, it will identify areas in which you could improve your learning.

Most of the research and writing about adult education indicates that there are four types of learners and learning. Different writers give different names to each type, but for easy recognition I have chosen the terms that Honey and Mumford use in their *Manual of Learning Styles*: activist; reflector; theorist; pragmatist. How do you know which type you are? Here is a short description of each. You may have trouble fitting neatly into one of them. You'll probably be mostly one but quite a lot of another and a little of each of the other two. If you really want to know more precisely, borrow Honey and Mumford's book from the library, complete the 80-question quiz and analyse it according to the instructions they give.

However, your initial reaction to the following outlines will probably be fairly accurate. We usually recognise ourselves because we usually feel that the way we operate is the best way. It's difficult for a pragmatist to understand why the theorist wants to do all that theorising, and why they don't just get on with the activity and see how it works out!

Activist

You'll try anything once. You act first and think later—if at all. You're open-minded and you like the challenge of new experience. You don't like the boring bits, the repetition and reflection which are necessary to real learning.

Reflector

You are cautious. You're the one who looks at everything from many different angles. You collect as much information as you can before you make up your mind about things. You are a good listener and like to be sure of what others are saying before adding your own ideas.

Theorist

You believe that if it's logical it must be good. You enjoy analysing and you're keen on systems, models, theories and principles. You want things to 'fit in' and you don't feel comfortable with lateral thinking or flippancy. You have strong beliefs about right and wrong, good and bad.

Pragmatist

You are practical, down to earth and keen to try out new ideas. You like to get on with things, try things out, see if they work in practice. You are a good listener, but you can be impatient to try out theories and techniques. You believe that if it works it's good.

Whose style?

At this point you need to think about this: most courses are presented according to the teacher's style, not the learner's style. This isn't to say that good teachers don't think about other styles, but they—almost subconsciously—tend to favour their own preferred style.

Having decided more or less which type you are, see whether the following information, under each heading, applies to you. Then check the suggestions for areas in which you could improve your learning.

Activists learn best when:

- There is something *new*.
- Activities are short, competitive and immediate.
- There is excitement or drama and a variety of activities to choose from.
- They are at the centre of things, leading discussions or giving presentations.
- No constraints or structure are imposed on the generation of ideas.
- They are challenged in some way, e.g. by adverse conditions.
- They are part of a team, solving problems, working with others.
- They are able to 'have a go'.

Where you need to improve your learning:

- Listening to lectures, explanations and instructions without wanting to rush off to try things immediately.
- Reading, writing and thinking on your own. A good exercise for activists is to keep a journal or diary, commenting on the day's activities. This gives you the

opportunity to write and think about what is happening in your life.

- Appraising what you have learnt—and this is where the journal comes in. It helps you think critically about what you have learnt each day.
- Practising the same activity over and over. Set a goal that's achievable: learn three new words each day for a week; keep practising them until you can use them with ease.
- Following precise instructions. Try out a new recipe without changing anything in it.
- Attention to detail. Practise something like drawing or listing all the items in a particular room (not the one you're in) you are familiar with. Then check to see how much you have 'seen'.

Reflectors learn best when:

- They can watch and think.
- They have time to prepare, to read some background material.
- They can investigate things.
- They have an opportunity to review things.
- They produce analyses and reports.
- They have a structured learning environment.
- There are no tight deadlines or pressure.

Where you need to improve your learning:

- When unplanned action is required. Try a spontaneous activity and just do it.
- When you have to base a conclusion on insufficient data. Make a list of the information you have, then try to guess the rest. Later, you can check whether you were right or not.
- When you are given precise instructions; try to follow them without looking for an explanation.

- When you have to take shortcuts because you don't have enough time. For a reflector this takes conscious effort, but try it some time anyway.

Theorists learn best when:

- They are presented with systems, models, concepts and theories.
- They can question the method and logic and check for consistency.
- They are intellectually stretched.
- The purpose is clear.
- Ideas and concepts are rational and logical even if they are not immediately relevant.

Where you need to improve your learning:

- In situations that involve emotions and feelings. When they come up, try to get in touch with how you feel about them rather than what you think about them.
- When you have doubts about the method or the information involved. Try to learn to take some things on trust. Ask yourself whether the person making the suggestion has credibility or not.
- When the subject seems shallow or gimmicky. You may sometimes need to look a little further to see what others see.
- When you feel out of tune with other students. If their learning styles and the teacher's style don't appeal to you, you may need to do some reading and research on your own to find the theoretical basis of the lessons or the course.

Pragmatists learn best when:

- The links between the subject and a problem are obvious.
- The subject has practical advantages.

- There is a chance to practise with feedback.
- They have an example or a role model.
- They can immediately apply what they have learnt.

Where you need to improve your learning:

- When you can't see an immediate use for the information. It pays to take notes and put them aside in case you can use them later, but it takes practice to do this.
- When there are no practical guidelines. A good exercise is to develop the guidelines yourself. They may even help other pragmatist students.
- When things seem to be going round in circles. Try looking more closely at the 'circles'; you may find that each one differs slightly from the last.
- When there is no apparent reward. Promise yourself small rewards for the goals you set yourself.

To get the best use out of all this information check which activities suit you best. In Chapters 9, 11 and 12 we look at how you can improve your learning by adapting both the lesson and yourself. Most important, be patient with yourself: it takes time and practice to adapt to new study methods as well as to adapt other styles to suit you.

3

Asserting yourself

IT ISN'T REALISTIC TO CRAM AN ASSERTIVE-
NESS course into one short chapter.
All I can hope to do is suggest some
strategies you can use and give you
a few examples of different ways of
saying things. Being assertive is not
the same as being aggressive
although sometimes it may be hard to see where one ends
and the other begins. The difference can best be summed
up by saying that assertive behaviour doesn't attack other
people.

Assertive behaviour involves knowing what you want,
believing that you have a right to it—or deserve it—and
then making this clear. This is not to say that you'll always
get exactly what you want. We all have to compromise, but
remember that this is not the same as giving in. The basic
rules of assertiveness are:

- Use I-language.
- Listen carefully.
- Be prepared to negotiate.
- Resolve conflicts as they arise.

If, up to now, you haven't been very assertive, changing
your approach may be a bit of a shock to the people around
you, so take it easy. Start small. Use I-language. Say what

you will or won't be doing or what you do or don't want. Don't tell the others what they should or shouldn't do: let them work it out for themselves. If they're more than 6 or 7 years old they should be able to work it out, even if they take a while.

You can develop an assertive belief system which will help you to behave more assertively and leave you feeling less guilty. The beliefs you develop may include some or all of the following:

- I'll do to others only what I would like them to do to me.
- I'll stand up for myself.
- I'll let people get to know me.
- I'll express my feelings honestly and directly.
- I'll try not to harm others because this will harm me.

Assertion involves standing up for your personal rights and expressing your thoughts, feelings and beliefs in direct, honest and appropriate ways that *do not violate another person's rights*. It also involves doing this without dominating, humiliating or degrading the other person. Assertion is about respect: that means respect for yourself and respect for the other person.

But how do you show respect when you refuse a request? The best way is to say quite calmly what you feel without making the other person feel bad for having asked. For example: 'I'd like to help you out, but I really don't feel comfortable around little kids.' The goal of assertive behaviour should be to give and get respect, to ask for fair play and to leave room for compromise when conflicts arise. This compromise means that each person will satisfy some of their needs.

Assertion is not just a way to 'get what you want'. This kind of thinking leads you to behave passively when you think you won't get what you want. It also concentrates only on what you want and not on other people's personal rights. And it could lead to the kind of irresponsible behaviour in which you take advantage of others.

Non-assertive behaviour

There are times when this seems to be the way to go. When you have to apologise, when you are unsure of yourself, when you would like to disappear. Don't be fooled, though. Non-assertiveness not only shows a lack of respect for yourself but it also shows a subtle lack of respect for another person's ability to cope with disappointment or responsibility. Non-assertive behaviour is also typical of people who want to avoid conflict at any cost.

Aggression

This type of communication is usually inappropriate, violates others' rights and is often dishonest. The usual goal of aggression is to dominate and win, which means someone else must lose. Here are some example situations and three ways you could respond to each one.

1 *Your teacher gives out much more work than necessary.*

The aggressive response: Mr Burns, you have a nerve giving me this much work. I know you're the teacher but I don't have to take this. You teachers think you can do what you like to the students. Well, you can't.

The non-assertive response: OK Mr Burns. I'll do it. You must have a reason for asking me to do all this . . . even if it isn't related to the classwork. I don't suppose you'd let me off this time?

The assertive response: Mr Burns, when you give me work

that's not related to your class I have to put in extra hours I don't have. So I have to say no to this extra work.

2 The person you are with has just made a sexist remark.

The aggressive response: Who the hell do you think you are? God's gift to women?

The non-assertive response: Oh, come on (haha), you know how much that irritates me when you say that (haha).

The assertive response: Frankly, I think that remark is an insult to both of us.

3 Trying to get a group back to the matter on hand.

The aggressive response: Can't you people get back to work and stop this goofing around?

The non-assertive response: I guess it's just my hangup. Do you think it'd be OK if we got back to the original subject? I've forgotten it myself (haha).

The assertive response: This is all interesting but we should get back to the original subject.

Of course a lot depends on the tone of voice you use, and you can make the assertive response sound aggressive if you speak loudly or forcefully. By keeping yourself calm and your voice soft, and saying things firmly but not forcefully, you'll make your point without upsetting people.

Conflict

When you learn to be assertive rather than aggressive or passive you become better able to deal with conflict. If you don't learn to handle conflict, and you aren't particularly assertive, you'll react in one of two ways: you'll become aggressive or you'll do your best to avoid the conflict. Neither method will solve the problem, and solving a problem is the only way to deal with it. So, with some assertive skills, let's look at the positive side of conflict.

Conflicts encourage change, and sometimes things need to change. We need to learn new skills, modify old habits, grow a little. All these can lead to conflict with the people around us. After all, they are growing and changing too, but usually in different ways, different directions and at different rates. Learn to be accommodating: give a little before you expect the other person to give, then negotiate outcomes that will satisfy both of you. And remember, good negotiation makes both parties feel OK—neither's a winner nor a loser.

Conflicts make life more interesting. Arguments about any topic make our interactions with people more intriguing and less boring. It's interesting to find out more about something when other people disagree with your ideas. We also make better decisions when there is disagreement between people responsible for making decisions because the conflict causes us to think about them more carefully.

A good argument can do a lot to clear away small day-to-day tensions that happen when people work or live together over a long period. The secret is to be able to end them amicably so there are no bad feelings left afterwards.

Conflicts can help you learn much about yourself: what makes you angry, frightened, what is important to you, and how you manage conflicts. You become aware of what you are prepared to argue about and what isn't worth the energy. But this learning process takes thinking about. Earlier, I suggested keeping a journal. When you've been in a conflict, make some notes of what it was about, how you felt, what you could have done better or just differently, how you might have managed a different outcome. It all then becomes a learning experience.

Last, but still quite important, conflicts can be fun if you don't take them too seriously. Think about the conflicts we set up deliberately with sports, games, movies, plays, books, and just by teasing each other. We all do this because we want that interaction with other people. We really are playful animals, but the play has to have an element of competition in it. But remember, there is a time when you do have to be serious. It's no good turning an argument with your superior at work into a play session: they probably take themselves much too seriously for that.

4

Goal-setting . . .

'Would you tell me please, which way I ought to go from here?'

'That depends a great deal on where you want to get to,' said the cat.

'I don't much care where,' said Alice.

'Then it doesn't matter which way you go,' said the cat.

Alice in Wonderland
Lewis Carroll

NOTHING UNDER THE SUN IS ACCIDENTAL. IF YOU DON'T SET YOUR OWN goals someone else will set them for you. Goal-setting is a bit like New Year resolutions: if they're too difficult to put into action they just don't happen. Where goal-setting differs from New Year resolutions is that you don't have to wait to make them, even if it's June. Goals are dreams and you can make them come true, but you must take some action.

How do you know what action to take? Well, it's a bit like planning a trip. You look at where you want to go and you decide on routes and transport. And remember, the fastest way isn't always the best! Build some review and revision into your study goals so the learning will be long-term and useful.

Like a well-run business, you should have long-term, medium-term and short-term goals. Having a long-term plan affects your day-to-day activities by helping you decide on the short-term goals instead of letting things drift along. Even if you aren't studying, you need a goal, just so you don't sit around watching TV for hours on end.

If you have a long-term goal, write it down. You can put it away and look at it again later—in a year or so—or put it somewhere so that you can see it every day. If, at the moment, you don't have a goal, list some of your dreams. Don't think of just the things you'd like to buy and own; perhaps you'd like to find a partner/spouse, or have a family, or change your career path, or learn a new leisure activity, or get a promotion at work. Keep this list handy and add to it over the next few days.

Goal-setting becomes very tied up with time management. You can really only plan *how* you'll spend your time when you know *what* you'll spend it on. Let's look at an example of how to set short-term and medium-term goals when we know what the long-term goal is.

Josie's long-term goal, now that her children are both at school, is to become a qualified engineer. This means a university degree, but because she left school at 16 and has no formal education, Josie is not very confident. But she is determined. Now in her late 20s, she realises that she still has about 30 or 40 years of working life ahead of her. She doesn't want to spend those years doing the same job she did when she left school. On the other hand, she really should get a job as soon as possible because she needs the money. So, let's look at what Josie can do in the short term and medium term to put her on track.

First, she will have to consider all the different branches of engineering and decide which interests her most. Then there are two other tracks she must investigate: which subjects are important, and what lower-qualified jobs are available in the engineering field she chooses? For instance, Josie is interested in civil engineering (the design and construction of roads, bridges, dams, railroads, airports, and so on). For the first question, she finds the most important subject is maths; for the second, the unskilled jobs are on building sites and usually filled by men.

Josie sets her first two medium-term goals as 'getting a job (any job) in the industry' and 'getting into university'. She would like to achieve these within the next two years. To give herself the confidence to get into university, she has to study maths and science, neither of which she did particularly well at in school. She must also find a job. So she now has two short-term goals: find a job and get into a maths and/or science class. The first step Josie must take for the maths and science is to decide where and how she'll study. Chapter 10 gives more details about learning centres.

Once Josie has found out about maths and science courses her next short-term goal is to get into the class or enrol in a correspondence course. Once she has done that her short-term goal will change again: she must get a pass mark or better for the course, and this can be narrowed down to completing the next assignment.

If we look a year ahead now, we find that Josie is doing well in her maths class, she's coping with the science class but she hasn't been able to find a job in the industry. One morning she finds in the newspaper an advertisement for a job as a lab worker—no experience necessary—with a company that does genetic engineering. If she applies for this job, and gets it, she will have to change part of her long-term goal.

Long-term goals are vital, but they should be flexible enough to take advantage of opportunities and learning experiences. This doesn't change the fact that the goals must be clear. When they are clearly and explicitly stated we have no trouble seeing whether we are heading in the right direction. To keep yourself on track, spend a few minutes every week reviewing your achievements. Don't dwell on anything that you didn't achieve: reschedule it or forget it.

All high achievers set goals. They not only know where

they're going, but they have a good idea of how they will get there. Note that I said 'a good idea': don't set your goals in concrete. Be ready to change them when the need or the opportunity arises. After all, the ultimate goal should be to have the best life you can.

The circle of self

Your subconscious mind probably doesn't distinguish between real and imagined experiences, so if you keep seeing yourself as a winner your subconscious will believe it and very soon you will be. It works like this: you create an image of yourself that pleases and satisfies you. Make sure it is fairly detailed. More important, make absolutely sure it is what you really want, not something you think someone else wants you to be, because it's a bit like programming a new computer. Once you put in a program and start running it, the longer you run it the harder it is to change.

This self-image you have programmed will determine how you perform. If you have a poor self-image you will expect to perform poorly, but if you program a good self-image you will expect to perform well. Either way, you'll live up to your own expectations. Doesn't it make sense to set up a positive rather than a negative program? You should expect to get the best from yourself and you will.

Having set up a good self-image and expectations of success you still have something else to do: you have to keep feeding the machine. The jukebox will keep playing only if you put coins in. What you have to do to keep yourself on track, on an upward spiral to success, is called 'self-talk'. What you say and think about your own performance will reinforce your self-image either positively or negatively. The most important item in this list is a positive mental attitude. If you've had a negative attitude for a long time it will be quite difficult to turn it into a positive one, but like a lot of other things we talk about in this book, you start with one small step. The next step will be a little easier and the one after that easier still.

From your positive self-talk, you get back to your self-image. Think positive and your self-image will improve, your performance will improve, and then your self-talk will become even more positive. More than that, though, the self-talk will become more believable and therefore more effective.

Improve your self-image

Your subconscious mind can't tell the difference between a real or imagined experience. So the more you imagine success the more your performance will improve because you are reprogramming your subconscious. Use phrases like 'I can do it'. Don't try to explain why you can't do something. Tell yourself that you can, that you'd like to have a go because you know you could do it if you try. The more you give yourself positive feedback the more you reinforce this image of successful achievement.

Use relaxation time—and the techniques in Chapter 7—to speed up the reprogramming process. When your body is relaxed your mind becomes even more receptive to this self-talk.

Are you reluctant?

There are several reasons why people are reluctant to set goals, but the main one is:

False
Evidence
Appearing
Real

The evidence is false but it appears real, and if it appears real it is real because we believe it.

- Some of us are afraid we'll fail.
- Some of us are afraid we'll be ridiculed.
- Some of us, surprisingly, are afraid of success.

Depending on which of these applies to you, try to imagine a 'worst case scenario'—the very worst things that could possibly happen if you fail, if you're ridiculed or if you're successful. Try to imagine this in as much detail as you can. Now, try to imagine, also in detail, how you would react to this. What would you do or say? What would happen after you do that? And then? Having imagined it, do you think you could live through the experience? Wouldn't it be easier if you didn't have this fear?

Most important, though, is to ask yourself how likely this terrible event is, and whether you could prevent it by following some of the advice and information in this chapter. The advice from some high achievers is:

- Be specific about your goals.
- Concentrate on seeing success wherever possible.
- Start to behave as though you are an achiever.

Some points to remember

1 Concentrate on two goals at a time.
2 Review your goals regularly to allow for change.
3 As soon as one goal is achieved, replace it with another.
4 You don't pay a price for achieving goals, you reap the benefits.
5 You pay for not having goals by feeling cheated out of opportunities you didn't take.
6 Improve your self-image. Remember, the better the image the stronger the motivation.

29

Finally, I'd like to introduce you to SAM because he knows all about goals. He knows that the secret of goal-setting is that all goals should be:

Specific
Achievable
Measurable

PART 2

Setting yourself up for study

5

Your time

EACH ONE OF US HAS A PARTICULAR TIME OF the day—or night—when we function best. Some of us are nightowls, some work best very early in the mornings, and some of us take half the day to wind ourselves up. Apart from deciding whether we are owls or larks we also need to look carefully at the things that currently occupy our time. Because we are basically 'doing' creatures we tend to fill our waking hours with activity. Once you make a decision to study you must realise that you are making a commitment that will take time, and time isn't something you can buy along with your books and equipment. The time you commit to your studies is time you will beg, borrow and steal from other areas of your life—from social duties, household chores, your family and your boss. And you'll promise to make it up at some other time and with luck and good management you probably will. But remember, when you eventually find the time your family may have made other commitments of their own.

There are heaps of books on time management and they use words like 'prioritise' and 'factor in' but the best advice I've ever heard was this: plan carefully and find a way that suits you best. One way is to set aside a fixed period (20–30 minutes) at the same time every day. Another is to plan blocks of time (2–3 hours) two or three times a week. In her first year of study Sue set aside half an hour every day but found that it made her feel as though she never had a day off. In her second year she changed over to 2-hour blocks twice a week and gave herself one full day off each week. She got just as much work done with much less stress.

The important thing is to be honest when you make this commitment. If you're going to spend an hour on something be sure it is a full measure. You'll only be cheating yourself if it isn't.

One advantage of studying at the same time every day is that it becomes a habit, a part of your routine. Another advantage is that the people around you know that is your study time and—if they know when it will end—will respect it. Of course, if you have young children it may not be so easy. If you have a spouse who is also studying, try to give each other the time you need.

Beware, though, of subtle forms of sabotage. The well-meaning spouse who constantly comes to 'see if you're OK' or brings in cups of coffee or tea probably doesn't even realise that they disturb you. One way to deal with this situation is to suggest, before you go to your books, that you will come out and have a cup of tea with them at a specified time that suits you both. Be definite, though, and don't have the cup of tea alone over your books. Take a break and spend 10 minutes away from your work, talking instead, and then go back feeling refreshed.

All this talk of time concerns, of course, your own study time and is additional to the time you will spend in classes or lectures, getting books from the library, meeting fellow students in study groups or for coffee and a chat. A good basis for calculating study time is 1:1—that is, 1 hour of study for every hour of lectures. For example, if you are doing a course that has a 2-hour class per week and you get into the habit of studying for half an hour every day you will be doing 3½ hours of independent study per week: almost twice the minimum.

You'll also need to improve your concentration span. Most of us these days have a concentration span of about 15–20 minutes. After that we begin to think about such things as 'how much longer do I have to do this?' or 'I should put a load of washing in the machine' or 'I wonder what X is doing now'. As a simple exercise to increase your concentration span, buy a small mechanical timer: one that has a dial to set the time and rings a bell when the time is up. Start off by setting it for slightly less than what you think your maximum concentration span is. Suppose you decide this is 20 minutes. Set out your work and decide what you will do: for example, read a chapter or write some notes. Set the timer for 18 minutes and start working. You don't have to check your watch or the clock because the bell will ring. If you start wondering when it will ring, then your concentration span is shorter than you thought. Check the time and stop working. Tomorrow, set the timer for one or two minutes earlier.

It's a bit of the Pavlov dog theory: you condition your mind to keep working until the bell rings, to focus on the work and not think about other things. With some practice you become so engrossed in your work that you may jump when the bell rings. When you get to this stage you begin very slowly to increase your study time—maybe by a minute or two every few days. Eventually you should be able to get to a full hour. When you do, give yourself a treat: go for a walk, sit quietly and listen to some music, have some fun—whatever turns you on.

Scheduling your time won't make you super-efficient: it's almost impossible to keep to a rigid schedule day after day. If you do try it and fail, you'll feel discouraged and be tempted to give up altogether. But there is a better way, one that still leaves room for those unexpected activities:

the three-part scheduling plan, which is recommended by many student counsellors because of its flexibility in the short-term application.

Step 1

Draw up a timetable of all your fixed commitments, which includes all those things over which you have little or no control, such as lecture times, work hours, meetings you must attend. Draw it up in some kind of visual form, perhaps like the example opposite.

This step is necessary only at the beginning of each semester: a good time to get things done because you'll find that your enthusiasm is usually at its highest during the first 2 weeks. Also, you'll find that your lecture times probably change each semester, as you do different subjects.

Step 2

This needs doing once a week and Sunday evening is usually a good time. You'll need to make a thorough list of the major events and amount of work you want to do during the week ahead. This list should contain not only study activities but everything of importance during the coming week. For example:

Concert Wednesday night
History assignment Thursday
Finish library search by Friday
Kate's birthday party Saturday afternoon
Eng. Lit. test Wednesday

The events on this list will change from week to week, that's why it's so important to make a new one each week.

	MON	TUE	WED	THUR	FRI	SAT	SUN
7.00							
8.00	Eng		Work	Hist	Work	Tennis	Tennis
9.00	"		"		"	"	"
10.00		Psych	"		"		
11.00			"		"		
12.00	Hist	Study group	"	Work	"		
13.00	"	"	"	"	"		
14.00		"	"	"	"		
15.00		"	"	"	"		
16.00			"				
17.00							
18.00							

Step 3

This is the short-term list: you'll do a new one every day. Use a small card or notebook, something that will fit into your pocket or purse. On this card list all the tasks you want to do that day. It could look something like this:

Review Eng. Lit. for test
Work on library search
Pick up party items from supermarket
Fetch clothes from dry cleaners
Set out snack for babysitter
Go to concert

This list should be as comprehensive as possible, to lessen the chance of forgetting something. As things get done, cross them off or tick them. If a task takes more time than you planned you can rearrange some of the other tasks, and the same thing applies if something takes less time. At the end of the day you can see what you have or haven't achieved. Sometimes uncompleted tasks can be moved to the next day; other times the opportunity has been missed. For the sake of your self-esteem try not to keep moving a task from one day to another. If you haven't done it the second time it's on your list, ask yourself whether you really want to do it and whether you really have to do it. Quite often you'll be surprised at the response.

If you're at the stage where you haven't enrolled in a course yet but are seriously thinking about it and wondering if you'll have the time, try the following. For the next seven consecutive days, keep a record of all the things you do in a day and how much time each one takes. At the end of the week, mark with a highlight pen all the items you think are so important that you simply couldn't avoid doing them. Then, with a different colour, highlight all the items you could leave out—all those things you do either to fill in time or because someone else has persuaded you to do them even though you don't particularly want to. You'll probably find that there are at least 5–6 hours that you could give over to study.

What it really amounts to in the end is how motivated you are. If you really want to do a course, you'll find the time, even if it's at 5.30 a.m. or staying up till way past midnight. I am constantly amazed at the sacrifices most of my students make to get their work done.

6

Your space

YOU'VE ENROLLED IN A COURSE AND HAVE begun to collect the first bits of paper, and if you keep them all—something we will discuss later—you will build up a surprisingly large collection in a short time. So, at this early stage it is really important to think about where and when and how you'll study.

Spaces and places

This section is for all of you who don't have any spare space to set aside as a study. At least half the mature-age students I have taught start with a shoe box and the kitchen table. Where you go from there depends on two main variables: how much space you can find, and what you are studying. For example, if you're learning cake decoration you'll need to use the kitchen; you'll also need somewhere to store a few books and your special equipment. Your products will be eaten—after you photograph them!—so they don't need storing for long. If you're studying literature at university you'll very soon need a fair-sized bookshelf and a desk.

Paper seems to be the common item: whether you are doing something as practical and material as pottery or as theoretical as philosophy, you will want to keep some kind of records. You will write down notes that a teacher gives you, ideas about your subject, essays that you hand in and then get back with marks and comments. There may be magazines or journals you'll want to keep; there will certainly be books you'll buy and keep. And if you're studying at any institution there will be some administrative paperwork like enrolment forms, receipts for tuition fees, student association dues, and so on.

For all the financial records you have to keep (you may be able to claim them on your tax return) the shoe box is perfect. Label it clearly, secure the lid and store it in a cupboard or under the bed. The reason for labelling it clearly is so that neither you nor anyone else doing some springcleaning will think it's just junk and throw it out. Officially, you're supposed to keep financial records for seven years.

Now, let's get back to those other things we mentioned: a place to put your books and writing paper. Take a walk round your home and see if there is anywhere you could put a small desk. My own desk is about a metre long and half a metre wide. It was bought for a child and has two small drawers. I graduated to this (after using a bureau in a corner of the hall for several years) when one of our children 'needed' a bigger desk.

With a small desk it's vital to have some storage space, and you could use a box under the desk. A small box could double as a footrest. You really do need somewhere to rest your feet when you sit for long periods at a stretch. Comfort has a lot to do with how long you spend at your studies. Plastic boxes—the ones that look like milk crates— hold an enormous amount but are small enough to make it easy to find what you want.

If there isn't any space for a desk, don't despair. Think, instead, of what you will be doing and you'll still find some alternatives: the kitchen table, a serving tray, a clipboard.

Where you study has a lot to do with how long you study for. The most important factors are comfort and ease of setting up. Physical comfort is most important. Make sure the place you choose is warm enough in winter (but not so warm that you fall asleep), cool enough in the summer, and well ventilated. Brain activity uses up a surprising amount of oxygen. You need fresh air and lots of it. If the room begins to feel stuffy, go for a short walk.

You also need a chair that you can sit on comfortably for quite a while. It must be the right height for your legs—or find something to put your feet on. If you don't have a box the telephone directories make a wonderful substitute. Ideally the chair should have a backrest, but it doesn't really need armrests. If your back doesn't rest on the back of the chair, try a cushion there because your back needs support. One of those little neck cushions, sometimes called peanut cushions, is ideal to put between the small of your back and the chair for support.

Other alternatives are the library—college, university or public. They all have quiet areas with tables or individual work places. One big advantage of working in the library is that any information you need will be at hand. The disadvantages are that you have to carry things with you, such as pens, notebooks, paper, etc., and that you will be out of contact with others, although this can be an advantage, too.

Don't just look inside the house for somewhere to study: you may be able to take a corner of the garage for yourself. You could put in a desk, a bookshelf and a lamp and put up a screen to enclose it. Or perhaps you have a garden shed where you can store your things, with a garden chair and table, but here you would be at the mercy of the weather. On nice days, though, it makes a wonderful change to take your books outside and sit in the garden or the nearest park to study.

If you have found a little space at home for a desk or

a bookshelf you may be able to put a corkboard on the wall above it. Once you start using it you'll wonder why you've never had one before. You can put up things that need attention, such as bills, and hang keys there—in fact, anything you don't want to file away and forget. There is one more essential item for your study area: a good lamp. Get one, if you can, that screws on to the edge of the desk (mine is fixed to the window ledge) and can be adjusted to the best angle for you.

If you haven't found any space for a desk, try a small suitcase or a large briefcase, a plastic crate or even a drawer in your clothes cupboard. The important point to remember is that it should be as quick and simple as possible to begin working, and just as quick and simple to pack it all up again when you stop.

All those papers

At the beginning of the chapter I mentioned all the paper you would collect. Not only the administrative forms, but all the lecture notes you make, the handouts you're given, the photocopies you'll make, the essays and assignments you'll write. You'll want to keep them all, at least until after the final exam. But my advice is to keep them even longer than that.

Unless you hated the subject so much that you are determined never to study it again, keep your notes and essays. When you go on and do the same subject at a higher or different level you'll have them to refer to. There is no need to keep re-inventing the wheel. If you've already done a library search or some of the research, use this material as a starting-point. It will save you time, but more important, it will refresh your memory of the subject and make it all a lot easier.

Remember, though, that this will work only if you have kept your notes orderly and in a dry place. If they're damaged or in a mess you'll get frustrated trying to find what you need, or you'll be sidetracked into reading a lot of interesting but irrelevant stuff and waste time.

The sound and the silence

Some of us like to study in peace and quiet, for others it is vital to have some music in the background. I'm a 'quiet' person but most of my household likes constant sound. If you like music, set up a tape or CD player near your study area. Experiment with different kinds of music for different moods and phases of your studies. Try some baroque—if you aren't familiar with it don't despair: I learned quite recently what it is. It's the right kind of music to alter your brain activity to alpha state, which is the state in which we do our best learning. Make sure you feel happy with the music you play.

To eat or not to eat . . .

Don't forget that you'll need food and drink regularly. It's better not to have it at your desk for several reasons: you don't want to spill things on your work; you need regular breaks from sitting; and you need the exercise of moving about for a few minutes. I try to have a break about every hour, even if I just have a glass of water and a walk around the house. When the weather's good I walk around outside the house, otherwise I just walk around the kitchen and the living-room. It's the movement that's important, and the mental break from the work.

Your space, like so many other aspects of your studies, is related to your motivation. If that's high you'll find enough space, just as you'll find enough time. We are, when we want to be, wonderfully adaptable. The best tool you can have to achieve your goals is determination. If you have that you can overcome just about anything.

7

Your health

STRESS IS ANYTHING THAT MAKES YOU uncomfortable, but we need to realise that not all stress is bad. Getting ready for a party you're looking forward to is stressful, but you don't feel stressed in the same way that you do just before a big exam or a job interview. It's impossible to avoid stress, and you really don't want to. What you do want is to avoid the bad stress.

So, what is stress? It's the state of arousal that gives your body the energy for tackling a situation. First and foremost, it's a condition of the mind, and sometimes we create our own stressful situations. It's your perception of an event that is important. Epictetus, in first century Greece, said: 'Men feel disturbed not by things, but by the views they take of them', suggesting that what happens to you is not as important as how you look at it.

Your immediate response to stress is physical, emotional or behavioural, depending on where you perceive the danger and how you have learnt to react. If you don't deal with the stress to ease it, you may suffer long-term effects. Stress that isn't resolved can cause problems in your job, your health, your family and your social life. However, stress can also help you achieve what you want to do. It brings anticipation and excitement into your life, helps you grow and change, avoid danger and strive for a goal. But you need to work out how much stress is right for you. You can be under-stimulated as well as over-stimulated. As stress increases so does performance and well-being until you reach your 'stress comfort zone'. Use stress management skills such as meditation and relaxation as you approach the point of over-stimulation.

Your personality influences the way you react and the way you are affected by stress.

Drs Friedman and Rosenman, in their book *Type A Behaviour and Your Heart*, suggest that there are two main types of personalities: Type A and Type B. Type As tend to thrive on negative stress, whereas Type Bs do not. Bs are more in control of themselves and the way they cope. None of us are ever totally A or totally B. We swing between the two, depending on the situation. The same situation can prompt different reactions from the same person, depending on the place, the time and their mood.

Are you an A or a B?

To get some idea, answer the following questions with a 'yes' or 'no'. Do you:

- Finish other people's sentences before they do?
- Move, walk or eat very fast?
- Prefer summaries to reading the whole article?
- Become angry easily in slow traffic?
- Generally feel impatient?
- Not notice details?
- Do two or more things at the same time?
- Feel guilty when you relax or take a holiday?
- Measure your work—and your worth—by salary, game scores or grades?
- Try to fit more and more activities into less and less time?
- Think about other things while talking to someone?

- Have nervous gestures like grinding your teeth, drumming your fingers or clenching your fists?
- Take on more and more responsibility?
- Accentuate 'key' words explosively when there is no need to do so?
- Hurry even when you don't need to?

More than ten 'yes' answers and you are definitely an A. Let's look at Type A characteristics because the Friedman and Rosenman study showed that Type A people were three times more likely to have coronary heart disease than Type B people. Now, I'm not suggesting that you can change your personality type just by reading this and changing your lifestyle—it's much more difficult than that. I'm suggesting that you try to modify some of your characteristics if you are a Type A.

Type A	**Type B**
Highly competitive	Easygoing
Aggressive and hostile	Patient
Extremely achievement-oriented	Not pre-occupied with achievement
Time-driven	Not driven by the clock
Does things fast	Not rushed
Perfectionist	More relaxed

This doesn't mean that Type B people don't get things done, but perhaps they enjoy things more and take time to smell the roses.

Negative stress

Stress-producing situations are all around us, and there is a well-established connection between stress and illness. But have you ever thought that there is also a connection between stress and wellbeing? Even really happy occasions can cause stress, so why don't they cause illness? The stress caused by happy events, enjoyable situations and successes you have worked hard for releases into your system a hormone that protects you from disease; bad stress, on the other hand, releases a different hormone, one that can cause problems in large doses. That's why a certain amount of stress is necessary, but not too much.

The difficulty is in knowing how much is too much. We all need some stress: it's what keeps us going, gives us our drive. Negative stress can be one of three kinds: physiological, psychological and situational. We'll examine them one by one.

Physiological

This is the kind of physical stress you get from sudden shocks and problems or from activities that demand more than your body can cope with. A good example of a physiological stress is a near miss on the road. You're driving and somebody pulls out of a parking spot. You slam on your brakes or swerve violently and avoid the accident. What you can't avoid is what happens to your body: your heart beats faster, and takes quite a while to slow down, your breathing is shallow and fast and you break out in a sweat. All these signs take time to return to normal. And the more often they happen, the more damage they do. Some of the long-term problems caused by this kind of stress are:

- stomach and bowel problems
- chronic skin problems
- smoking and drinking which lead to other ills
- tension headaches
- high blood pressure.

Drugs may help for a while but they merely mask the reaction. Over a period of time drugs actually increase stress. There are better ways! Let's look at them:

48

Music

This is a very personal thing. Some people prefer Mozart, others prefer Metallica; preferences also depend on our feelings at the time. To relax we need music with a slow beat to slow our heartbeat, but to get the housework done we need music with an upbeat tempo, to get us moving, lift our heartbeat and motivate us. But don't feel you must have music: some of us actually relax better in silence.

Aroma

This can affect the way you feel, physically and emotionally. You can use oils for

- bathing
- inhaling
- massaging
- vaporising.

If you've never tried oils before, start slowly. Just two or three drops in a bath or on a hanky will be enough at first. If you're using a vaporiser make sure the room is well ventilated. Aroma, like music, is not for everyone. Try one of these and see if you like it: basil, clary sage, frankincense, geranium, juniper, lavender, lemon, orange, sandalwood.

Meditation and relaxation

These are two more ways to heal your body when stress gets out of hand. Here are a few rules to start you on your relaxation program.

1   Find a place where you won't be disturbed by sudden noise or movement.
2   Choose a timeslot you can set aside every day—but not immediately after a meal or heavy exercise. First thing in the morning or last thing at night are both good.
3   Find somewhere comfortable where you can relax

muscle tension but not fall asleep. A beanbag or an armchair are good, or you could learn to relax by sitting on the floor, legs crossed, back straight.

4   To occupy your mind, choose an image, word or phrase to focus on.

5   Get yourself into the right frame of mind. You can't make yourself relax but you can allow it to happen. Your mind will stray but you should learn to return easily and often to your focus.

6   You must also be willing to practise regularly. They say it takes 21 days to form a habit, so at first it may seem difficult, but keep practising. It's worth it in the end.

Once you've arranged all these, start with 10–15 minutes a day. Sit down and concentrate on your breathing. Take a deep breath and let it out slowly. As you breathe out imagine the tension leaving various parts of your body. If this is difficult, try this: as you breathe in, move your fingers a little, then tense them; then, as you breathe out, feel them relax. Do this with all the other parts of your body and don't forget your face and neck!

Psychological

This is one we impose on ourselves. Often we have expectations of ourselves that are almost impossible to reach, and then we become unhappy when we don't succeed. Ask yourself these questions to see if you're actually punishing yourself:

- Do you feel guilty about relaxing?
- Do you become hostile easily?
- Do you always hurry?
- Do you focus on the outcome rather than the process?
- Do you hold on to your worries?
- Do you try to do lots of things at once?
- Do you read the headlines rather than the comics?

More than three 'yes' answers and you are definitely pushing yourself too hard. If you can't seem to relax or slow down on your own, find a yoga or relaxation class. Ask your doctor about classes in the area, but don't ask the doctor for 'tablets to help me relax'. If the doctor doesn't know about classes, your local library is sure to have information about courses and classes, as well as tapes and videos that will take you through relaxation exercises and get you started.

8

Your relationships

THIS CHAPTER IS FOR THOSE PEOPLE WHO HAVE decided for themselves that they would like to learn something. If you're attending a course because your employer wants you to do it, you should still read it, but you probably won't be able to follow some of the suggestions.

Seventy-five per cent of mature-age students are in long-term relationships. When I first became a student—at the age of 40—I came across a piece of information I found both interesting and frightening: approximately 50 per cent of mature-age students go through a relationship breakdown while they are studying. At that time I had been married for 14 years and had three young children. I was frightened by these statistics because I knew I didn't want to risk losing my family.

It wasn't easy ever, but another 15 years on my family is still intact. Sometimes the going was very hard, other times easier, but always in my mind were the people in my classes who were not doing so well. Worst of all was that the further we got into the course the more traumatic were the breakdowns. People had become so engrossed in their studies they were not even aware of how much they were neglecting their families. In most cases, when a spouse walked out the student hadn't noticed any of the signs. The shock was usually the hardest thing to deal with. And then resentment: 'This isn't fair, just before an exam (or when a major assignment is due, or whatever)'.

Before the problems arise

Whatever your reason for studying, start slowly. There are several very good reasons for this, but the most important one is your relationship. Don't take a big bite: a little one is always easier to chew. Enrol in just one subject in your first year or semester. Another reason for starting slowly is that, as an adult, you have so many other commitments.

Think carefully about what you are prepared to give up. Make sure you take your family with you on your journey of learning and discovery. If you do, you will all benefit from the experience. Children will be impressed and follow your example provided you don't push. If you are enjoying your studies and not stressing out over them, the kids will do the same. And talking to your partner about what you are doing, why you feel you want to do it and how it will benefit you and your partner all help to ease the way. In return, of course, you have to allow them some freedom, too.

Stress management

These days the first thing we think about when someone mentions emotional health is stress management. Stress itself is not really the problem: adrenalin is the hormone that gets us moving. Too much of it, though, like too much of anything, is what's bad. When we have no goals, no deadlines, we develop a 'mañana' attitude: why do today anything you can put off till tomorrow? The opposite of this is the old saying that a busy person always finds time to do more. It's about momentum: once you get going it's easier to keep going. But we also have to look at our own limits and, in the end, learn to say 'no'. What you have to decide is who or what you will say no to, and then stick by your decision.

So, how do you decide? First of all, list—on paper or just mentally—the three most important things in your life. My first list, years ago, was my family, my work, my writing; studying was going to be a very part-time thing and it would be the first to go if there was any problem.

When you've listed three things, write them in order of importance on a small card and keep it where you'll see it often. By the end of the semester you'll need it, because that's when the pressure begins to increase, subtly but surely, especially if you have exams. By the middle of the second semester my list had changed to family, study, work. The writing came a long way after that. Over the next few years it was often a struggle to keep 'family' and 'study' from changing places. Other students told me they were having the same problems. Listening to how they were dealing with them was helpful, even when they were not successful: you could tell yourself what to avoid as well as what would work.

One of the more successful strategies involves the time management plan described in Chapter Six. Planning ahead is the very best way to cope, but don't fill in so much that there's no room to be spontaneous. After all, we have to remember that Jack and Jill need to play as well as work, and play isn't play when it's programmed. On the other hand, a lot of the things we need to do for and with our families don't fit into that spontaneous category. Birthdays, anniversaries and traditional festivities happen at fixed times and you should be able to pencil them into your yearly planner at the beginning of the year.

As mature-age students we are involved in adult education and the primary difference between this and school education is that the students have more responsibility for their own learning and more freedom to negotiate work-loads and attendance patterns.

One good way to deal with the possibility of absence from class is to set up a 'buddy system'. In this system, you team up with another student or two and arrange to take notes and collect handouts for one another when one of you misses a class for some reason.

The way we feel about our family relationships is affected by our cultural background, our previous experiences, our perspective, the partner relationship we have, and the status of that relationship.

Many mature-age students are women and many come from cultural backgrounds where women have very restricted areas of activity. In most cultures problems arise when women are better educated or in any way appear to have higher status than their husbands. The movie *Educating Rita* was released when I was in my second year of study. The conflict between Rita and her husband is just as true today as it was then. One way to deal with this situation is to encourage your partner to study as well, but this could backfire if their studies then become 'more important' than yours. It seems always to come back to the level of communication between individuals. Almost all problems seem to be solved by using good communication techniques: by talking things through and listening carefully to one another.

Defusing the conflict

If conflict-prone situations are dealt with at a very early stage there is a good chance that the conflict will be avoided. The basic causes of marital and family conflicts can probably be counted on one hand:

- money—how it's coming in or how it's going out
- time—what's getting done and what's not
- attention—who's getting it and who feels they're not.

How the members of any household handle these issues will vary widely.

The most common cause of trouble is that one or more people feel neglected. If you are wife and mother in a traditional family your role, whether you like it or not, is seen as that of nurturer, sounding-board, shoulder for crying on, sympathetic ear, source of advice, organiser—and usually doer—of household chores, and about fifty other things beside. Now, because you've decided to study, you suddenly find you can't cope with all these demands. Don't wait for the crisis: do something as early as possible! Start by sharing your plans with everyone you think will be affected. Not just the members of your immediate household; if you're in the habit of phoning an elderly parent every day for a long chat, tell them your plans.

A word of warning here, though: as surely as the sun will rise, you will find at least one person who will try to discourage you. *Don't listen to them.* Read Chapter 3 to learn how to deal with them—assertively. As well as discussing your plans, share your goals with them. Explain exactly what motivates you. Enlist their help in keeping you on track. Ask them to remind you of these goals when you become disheartened or depressed—it will happen.

Once you've passed this stage, the next step is easier—but only a little easier. Explain, when you've enrolled and you have your timetable, what time you will have for them and what time you will need for study. Do it in that order: first them, then your studies. Then ask each member of the household to nominate one way in which they think they could help you to achieve your goals. Don't think that you will cope with the extra workload, unless you normally watch 5–6 hours of television a day and want to break the habit.

Think of it this way if you have kids: teaching them early in life that household chores are not gender-specific will make them better adults and better partners. Also, practising democracy at a family level will make them better citizens. Try to have a family meeting—call it a council—about once a month, and don't be afraid to give even 5-year-olds some responsibilities. You'll be surprised how they'll blossom. Responsibilities make us feel needed and we all want to feel needed.

Constructive conflict

Here are four things you can look for to tell you whether the conflict has been constructive:

1   If the relationship is stronger, and you are better able to interact or work with each other, the conflict has been constructive.
2   If you like and trust each other more, the conflict has been constructive.
3   If you are both satisfied with the results of the conflict, it has been constructive.
4   If you have improved your ability to resolve future conflicts with one another, the conflict has been constructive.

9

Identifying personal blockages

 BLOCKAGES COME IN THREE VARIETIES: procrastination, lack of motivation and what Stephen Brookfield calls 'the imposter syndrome'. Most of us suffer from each of these at some stage, so we'll look each one in the eye and learn to deal with it. Just one word of warning: don't try to eliminate them all completely. A little procrastination, used wisely, can be a good anti-stress device. As for the other two, just when you think you've got them beaten they'll pop their heads up somewhere else, so you need to keep watching for them.

Procrastination

Instead of sitting down and writing this chapter I have, this morning, made three phone calls, looked for a book someone asked me about, gone out twice to check the mailbox and done several household chores which other members of my household would have done. *That* is procrastination. Oh, yes, I also read almost all the P-words in my dictionary.

Why did I do it? Believe me, I ask myself that every time it happens. However, I can justify some of these activities. For example, since I haven't spoken to my father-in-law for more than a week I really should just call to see if he's OK. Then I phoned a colleague to explain something quite insignificant. And while I was making phone calls, I decided to call a friend to invite her over the week after next. I couldn't make it next week because—panic, horror—this manuscript is due at the publishers then. Of course it'll be ready . . . well, it may be a day or two late . . . or a week . . . It's not that I don't want to do it but . . .

The truth is that the writing is scary. What if I can't think of anything to write? What if it all just turns out to be garbage? What if Joshua (my publisher) thinks it's rubbish? What if my kids think it's just stupid? Most of our worries start with 'what if . . .' and we spend time worrying about things that will probably never happen and if they did it wouldn't really matter. I hate housework and I love writing, yet quite often I find myself doing chores to avoid sitting down at my desk. Some strategies that can help include the following.

Breaking down all tasks into very small steps

You can then tell yourself you will do just one of these. That shouldn't be difficult. If you're the sort of person who is motivated by good outcomes, visualise the whole task completed and then think how much this step will help you get there. If, on the other hand, you are motivated by avoiding negative consequences, remind yourself what will happen if you don't complete the task. Either way you are more likely to break the barrier by taking small steps.

Setting aside fixed blocks of time for each area of your life

This one is based very much on self-discipline: if you promise yourself you will do something—housework, study, visit, whatever—for an hour on Tuesday, you have to keep that promise. Most people find this one quite difficult.

Planning everything ahead

Most times procrastination is an outward sign of stress. We have to recognise avoidance tactics for what they are: they indicate that the task is causing stress, and once we examine its real cause we will be in a better position to deal with it.

Jenny felt guilty about studying. Her 18-month-old son took up a lot of her time, but not all. She and her partner had agreed that she wouldn't go back to a full-time job until the baby went to pre-school. Meanwhile, Jenny had enrolled in a course to help her get a better—or different—job. When the baby was very small Jenny had managed to finish the assignments for her course on time and still keep the house to her own high standards. As her son grew bigger, noisier and more active Jenny found she had less time for her studies. When she did sit down to work she felt guilty about other things she thought she should be doing.

Jenny's help finally came from her mum, who pointed out that some of the chores could be done less often and others could be done as a game, getting the toddler to help. Once Jenny confronted her guilt and discussed it with her partner she began to deal with it. She still feels bad when she leaves the baby and his father to do their own thing on a Saturday or Sunday, but she is much happier about having turned 'tidy-up time' into a game that her son, now almost two, plays with gusto.

If your kids are a little older try good old bribery—except these days it's called negotiation: 'I'll drive you to Joey's place if you mop the kitchen floor while I fold the laundry.' Leave room for negotiation. My kids would have said, 'I'll fold the laundry instead', and we would have come to some agreement. Be sure, though, that you agree on when as well as what will be done. When it comes to studies, try saying, 'I'll help you with your school project if you'll help me with mine.' This works two ways: by trying to explain what you are studying to a child of anything from 8 upwards means you will have to really understand it yourself. You'll clarify things in your own mind. The other benefit—which I didn't understand for years—is that your children and your spouse will come to understand not only what you study but also how you feel about it.

Lack of motivation

Motivation is directly related to goal-setting, which we talked about in Chapter 4. A goal is a tremendous motivator but every so often we lose sight of our goals, especially if we tend to focus on the long-term goals. It is the short-term goals that give us the energy to get through the next hour, day, week . . .

Long-term goals are usually too big and difficult to reach in one leap. Better to watch where you have to put your foot down next than to focus on the mountain-top and fall in the river. On the other hand, if you lose sight of the mountain-top altogether you won't know where the next step ought to be. It all comes down to goal-setting and good planning.

If you seem to lose your motivation often or for long periods try some positive self-talk. Remind yourself why you started, what you hope to achieve, what it will feel like when you get there. If necessary, write your goals on cards and put them on your noticeboard, on the wall, on the front of some of your books, anywhere you'll see them often.

Sometimes a lack of motivation in one area—your studies—is caused by a surge of activity and enthusiasm in another area. Starting a new job, for instance, could lower your enthusiasm for your studies. Give yourself a short time to settle in, then go back to your plans for study and look at starting with the small steps I mentioned earlier in this chapter. Another way to revive your motivation is to study with a friend. It is unlikely that you will both suffer from the same degree of lack of motivation at the same time.

The imposter syndrome

This phenomenon, which is far more common than you would think, shows itself in our feelings about our own 'worthiness'. We feel that we shouldn't really be here; that someone in the enrolments office made a mistake and put our name on the acceptance instead of the rejection list; that all the other students know so much more than we do and that any minute now a teacher or administration staff member will discover the mistake and we'll be asked to leave. This may not seem like an important issue from a learning point of view, but it is. It inhibits your learning because you don't give the studies your full attention. You're constantly worrying about how you compare with all these other bright students. You don't ask questions for fear that you'll sound foolish. After all, you tell yourself, the other students probably all know the answer to that one.

The best way to deal with the imposter syndrome is to make a note of all your successes. Remember, you have a whole lifetime of experiences to draw on. The bright young students in the class probably feel inadequate, too, even when they speak as though they know it all. And if you have a teacher who puts the students down, who is supercilious and sarcastic, then all you can do is to tell yourself that the teacher has a problem, too.

A good teacher, one who empathises with the fears and doubts of mature-age students, praises where it's due, reserves the criticism and makes it constructive. But most teachers will probably not even notice your feelings and will think that you are not participating as fully as you could. If I have convinced you that much of your learning depends on you and what you do, then the imposter syndrome is something you will be able to deal with.

Talk to other students. You'll probably be surprised to find that quite a few feel the same and have very similar problems. Discuss the teacher's behaviour: which aspects of it make you feel better and which make you feel worse? You could form a mutual praise group, to boost each other's morale. You may even be able to discuss the problem with particular teachers in an assertive, non-threatening way, but this can be quite difficult.

All in all, blockages happen to all of us for different reasons and at different times. Realising this right from the beginning means that when they occur, you can do the following things:

1 Keep your goals firmly in sight.
2 Take precautions by studying with a friend.
3 Ask family members to be supportive and encouraging.
4 Go back to small, easily achievable tasks.
5 Review your goals.
6 Remember SAM from Chapter 4: make those goals Specific, Achievable and Measurable.

PART 3

Getting the most out of your study

10

Making the right choices

WHEN YOU ENROL IN A SUBJECT YOU already know something about you go into your first class with some background—the teacher/lecturer presents basic information that you have a nodding acquaintance with. That means you sit in the first session nodding your head, saying to yourself, yes, I know that, and that, and that. All this gives you confidence so that when the teacher presents the first new piece of information you are not too overwhelmed.

Success is like a spiral: you go up step by laborious step, but if you stop, it's hard to keep your place. Sliding down is a rapid process. Success also boosts your self-esteem and confidence, and as your confidence goes up so does your success rate.

Educational providers range widely, from neighbourhood centres to universities, and if you haven't done any kind of formal learning since you left school—and if that was a long time ago—the neighbourhood centre may be the best place to start. It's wonderful to see adults blossom and gain the confidence to go further along the road to the education they missed earlier in their lives. Not that everyone needs to go through the rigours of university. Education should lead to self-fulfilment and satisfaction. It seems to me that if your only goal is to earn more money, then an arts degree is probably not the right way to go. But if you want a satisfying life and to enjoy each day for what it brings then the neighbourhood centre may be the way to go.

Neighbourhood centres

These are sometimes called leisure learning centres, and most operate only one day a week. Their teachers are usually volunteers who have a passion for their subject and whose teaching styles vary a great deal, which can be an advantage. Because they are enthusiastic about their topic this enthusiasm is passed on to their students.

Don't underestimate what these centres can offer: they go far beyond the art and macrame classes. Those I've been involved in have run courses ranging from astronomy (the teacher was an astronomer on the staff of the Australian Radio Telescope), to creative writing, history, languages, philosophy and zoology. Classes are informal, there are no exams, no certificates and the cost of attending is usually very low. This, if you can do it, is the gentlest re-entry to education.

Because the cost is low you can sample several subjects before you decide to go further. My own introduction to this system came about because I volunteered to teach a needlework class. At that stage I had no teaching qualifications but I loved my craft. For me it led, eventually, to a degree in Adult Education.

Community colleges

These used to be known as evening colleges and almost every suburb had one. Now they have changed their name, run classes in the daytime, even on weekends, and focus more on business and industry. You will find all the traditional hobby courses and much more, but you'll also find that courses are priced accordingly.

The standard of teaching is mostly on a par with the leisure learning centres but the equipment and facilities are much, much better. Some of the courses give you a certificate of attainment to show what you have studied, but employers' acceptance of them varies. One of the advantages these colleges have over neighbourhood centres is that they tend to hold classes at more convenient times for students who have full-time jobs. Some people choose a subject just because it's on the 'right' night or because a friend wants to do it and is too shy to go alone. Quite often that's fine and students develop an interest in something they may never have thought of trying on their own. But to get the most out of a course you really should choose something that interests you from the beginning.

The WEA

The Workers' Educational Association (WEA) is an independent body which provides a wide range of educational activities from single lectures to 25-week courses and overseas study tours. Teachers all have sound subject qualifications and take part in teacher training. According to their brochure the WEA

> . . . seeks to ensure that the study of the social and natural sciences, of history and current affairs, of the humanities, etc., be a cooperative activity between students and tutors, informed by free discussion and a critical examination of opposing points of view—avoiding all forms of indoctrination and propaganda.

Courses begin at various times throughout the year and there are workshops, seminars and lectures happening all the time. A phone call to their Sydney office will get you a brochure—*WEA Sydney: What it is, What it does, How it works*—and the latest program.

Except for some special computer and business oriented courses, the WEA doesn't usually give certificates, but for a small additional fee when you enrol, they will issue one at the end of a course.

TAFE

Technical colleges are becoming more and more industry-oriented. Except for their rapidly shrinking General Studies sections, they are geared to give trade education. You can do a course there part-time, which means that you would probably have to attend evening classes, but some are held only during the day.

TAFE teachers are a mixed bag: some very good and some appalling, with most somewhere in between. Beware, especially, of evening classes. They are frequently taught by part-time teachers who have already done a full day's work in another job. They may have no teaching qualifications, or they may be school teachers, and they are not supervised by head teachers. If you have any doubts about a teacher's performance talk to the Head of Studies at the college. For more information on teachers and teaching methods read Chapter 12.

One more tip about TAFE: if you really want to go to university, don't ask the TAFE college how to go about it. Most of the mature-age students I have met were told by TAFE that they first had to do a 2-year HSC course. This is not true, and doing the HSC puts most mature-age students at an unnecessary disadvantage because they have to compete with thousands of 18-year-olds for university positions, whereas most universities these days have a separate quota for mature students.

Most TAFEs do, however, offer a Tertiary Preparation Course, which runs for 1 year and teaches research skills, essay writing, maths and some elective subjects. But check out the universities. Most of them offer good support systems for mature students. They offer study skills courses, counselling units and other facilities to ease you into the system.

Universities

Take a good look around before you make your final decision. Some are easier to get into, some offer courses the others don't have, some have more prestige, some offer distance (correspondence) learning, some have summer schools, some offer non-award courses. Most, these days, have child care facilities, but they are usually heavily booked. Check early if you need them. Some will allow you to begin with a reduced load, meaning that you can do just one or two subjects in the first year. Most unis have a limit on the number of years you can take to finish a degree: the average is 9 years to complete a 3-year full-time course. Don't be put off by that. It doesn't matter if it takes that long, although most people finish in about 5 years. Easing in slowly, doing only one subject the first year gives you the confidence to take on more in later years. It also gives your family a chance to adjust to the new situation.

Non-award courses

Some universities will allow you to enrol in one subject— most courses run for a semester, although there are also full-year courses—at the end of which you sit an exam or hand in an assignment, and receive a mark. When results are posted you'll get a letter to say that you've done the course. This is intended to give you a taste of university life and if you then decide to enrol in a degree course this subject will be counted in the number of units you'll need for the degree.

Summer schools

Because the summer vacation at university is 3 months long,

most have summer schools. The subjects they offer vary considerably and so does the standard of teaching, but this is another way to get an idea of what university study is like.

Distance learning

This used to be called 'correspondence courses' and there are still private correspondence colleges offering an enormous range of subjects. TAFE has expanded in this area and now offers a wide range of courses through its External Studies Department.

Several universities also offer this service. Some of these courses are done entirely by correspondence, others combine external work with short courses at residential schools. For example, at the University of New England you have to attend residential school for 4–5 days for each subject, and one or two weekend seminars. These residential schools consist of intensive lectures and are held at times when internal (full-time) students are on holiday: Easter, mid-winter and September. It's a bit like learning in a pressure-cooker but there is also time for some fun, and you get to meet other students doing the same subject. Without residential schools I would have found this kind of study very lonely.

Weekend seminars take place in various larger centres, such as Sydney, Melbourne or Brisbane, which are readily accessible to students from the surrounding areas.

Open university

These are the lectures broadcast on radio and television and you can find out more about how to enrol in them from your weekly television guide. Like correspondence courses, they are great if you cannot attend classes because you have a job, or for some other reason. If you're a 'visual person', or one who learns best by hearing, this is a step up from the traditional type of correspondence course that involves only written work.

Broadcast courses also give you a chance to sample a few different subjects before you make your final choice. The problem, though, is that you really need a video recorder because not all the lectures will be broadcast at a time to suit you.

11

Learning to learn

There are one-story intellects, two-story intellects and three-story intellects with skylights. All fact collectors who have no aim beyond their facts are one-story men (and women). Two-story men (and women) compare, reason, generalise, using the labour of fact collectors as their own. Three-story men (and women) idealise, imagine, predict— their best illumination comes from above the skylight.

Oliver Wendell Holmes

WHETHER WE LIKE IT OR NOT, MOST OF THE INFORMATION WE USE WHEN we study is found in books. So, the most important skill we need is reading, and the ability to understand what we read. At school we are taught to read words, but have you thought that you also learned to read pictures?

Being able to read pictures and maps is different to being able to read words. And reading words in one language doesn't automatically mean you can read everything you see. There are also other things we can 'read', like diagrams, sign language, animal tracks, weather signs and a few more.

We all have more than one way of knowing things. Some of us find learning easier one way, and some of us another way. You may remember doing IQ tests in school somewhere between the ages of 8 and 11. One reason why those tests were discredited was that they only measured your ability to read and your knowledge of the mainstream culture.

What we need to realise when we think of different ways of learning is that there are also different ways of teaching. Teachers feel most comfortable with their preferred learning style. For example, I'm a pragmatist and like to see how I can use the things I learn. When I teach I tend to give lots of examples but not much of the underlying theory. And I've found that the longer I teach a particular course, and the more familiar I am with the subject, the more I slip back to this method. So teachers who are completely familiar with their material generally tend to teach in their own preferred learning style. In this chapter I will show you some other ways of 'knowing' and some other ways of learning.

An overview

The two most common methods of learning in Western culture are the verbal system, based on language, and the logic system, which is mainly mathematical. Another way we have of knowing the world involves seeing spaces, designs, shapes and other information in a non-verbal visual form. Other kinds of knowledge include movement, gesture and action; music and rhythm; and two 'people-oriented' ways: inter-personal and intra-personal.

Because these different ways of knowing will open such wide horizons for you I have included exercises you can do to help you increase your own ways of learning.

Life's sentences

When we communicate face-to-face, body language and gestures convey a great deal of our message. When we use

75

any other form of communication we rely almost totally on words. So, if we use a word that doesn't mean exactly what we want to say, we have a problem. Putting words in the wrong order can sometimes sound funny, but can also cause real difficulties. We know—because we learned this in our first 5 years of life—that language has a definite pattern and structure. For example, if you find a list of words like this: 'bit the the man dog' you would have no trouble making the sentence: 'the dog bit the man'—or, as a joke, 'the man bit the dog'. Look at some other sentences and see how the meaning changes when words are moved to different positions. What about sentences you have written? Are they clear? Try changing some of the words. Add an adjective or an adverb, or take some out. Does the sentence flow better? Is the meaning clearer?

Motivation and persuasion

When we think of this kind of language we often associate it with politicians and lawyers, but children are good at it, too. Another word for it is 'rhetoric' and it has to sound convincing. Salespeople practise it every day. Can you persuade people? Try these exercises:

- Make a list of 10 reasons why people should save all the dust and fluff from filters in their clothes dryers.
- Write a radio or television advertisement to convince people to buy hamburgers made of sawdust.

Teach someone

We teach by explaining, by giving instructions the other person can understand. Not only must we be precise with the language we use, we must also take care not to miss out any of the steps. As an exercise to help you improve this skill, find a partner and give only verbal instructions for:

76

- sharpening a pencil
- sewing on a button
- pruning a rosebush
- any other reasonably complex action you can think of.

If you need to 'practise' the action to help you explain it, turn your back so your partner can't see you.

Now try this exercise: write the instructions for making a pot of tea for someone who has never made one before. Be sure you don't assume that they know any part of the procedure. Then ask someone to follow your written instructions.

Be funny

Sometimes we joke around with things we are learning and years later find that we remember not only the information but also the jokes and the fun. An easy form to use is a limerick or a verse of some kind. Limericks are short and have a basic structure. They are easy to write and easy to remember. The first and second lines rhyme with each other; the third and fourth lines rhyme with each other; and the fifth line rhymes with the first two, like this:

> There was an old lady from Cork
> Who tried to teach fishes to walk
> When they tumbled down dead
> She grew weary and said,
> 'Now I'll try teaching lobsters to talk'.

Make a list of words that relate to a subject you are learning and write a limerick using some of them.

Thanks for the memory

Memories are wonderful: we all have a lifetime's worth. But access to them when we need them is not always easy. If you keep a diary when you are young, it will keep you when you are old, or so the saying goes. It will certainly give you practice in expressing yourself. To begin with, write down in a notebook three of the day's events that you'd like to remember; three things you thought about; and three good things you did. Keep it simple. Write as much or as little as you want but do it each day for about 3–4 weeks: remember it takes 21 days to form a habit. At the end of the 3 weeks look back at the first few entries. Has it become easier for you to express yourself? Is your writing more fluent? More descriptive? During the day do you make mental notes to enter something in your journal? Start adding another item: perhaps one thing you learned today. See how long you can keep the journal going.

How many problems can you solve?

People are problem-solvers. It's what really makes us different from other animals. When we don't have any problems to solve we even go looking for some. And our education system has been built on logical thinking and problem-solving skills.

Problem-solving ranges all the way from calculating your change at the checkout to finding a cure for cancer. There are several kinds of mathematical intelligence: we can recognise abstract patterns; we can piece together clues to give a big picture; we can start with the big picture—a general rule—and work out the details; we can work out connections and relationships; we can do complex calculations even when no numbers are involved—for example, by using people, situations and events; we can also examine things and make deductions and predictions. Think about the complex calculations you do every time you cross a busy road or drive a car in traffic.

Next time you are with a group of people—in a meeting or a social group—listen to the conversation. Watch people's behaviour and their reactions to what is happening. Then see if you can predict what will happen next. Keep trying: very few people get it right the first time and some of us never get it right but at least you can come close.

Then try the exercise with something you're reading. If it's a short story, see if you can predict the ending after reading about a quarter, then a half, then about three-quarters of the story. Did you base your predictions on your own experiences? On other stories you've read? On other information you've picked up along the way? All these are valid and because they're inside your head they are yours to use. And this applies to all things we know and do.

Once you've had some practice at predicting, try to use it in lectures by reading some of the textbook before the lecture and then listening for new information from the teacher. Learning is an active process. It's something you do, not something that's done to you.

Here is a series of activities to help you apply logical thinking to reading comprehension. Choose a familiar piece that you understand thoroughly—something with about 10–12 paragraphs.

- Number the paragraphs and then, on another page, write key words to remind you of what each paragraph is about.
- Look at these key words and divide them into two parts.
- Give each part a title that describes what's happening.
- Give the whole piece a title (or a new title if it already has one).

Now, using the same piece of reading do this:

- Draw two large circles overlapping one another as shown in Figure 1 (this is called a Venn diagram and is useful for any comparisons we want to make).
- Choose from the piece two things for comparison: two characters, or two situations or two jobs.
- Where the circles overlap, write all the similarities.

Figure 1 Venn diagram

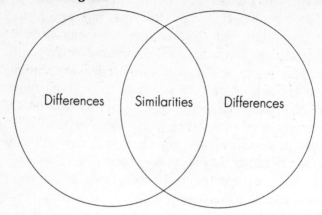

Differences   Similarities   Differences

- In the other areas, write down all the things that are different.

You may have to guess some of the things according to what you know.

Another exercise that will help you to look for information is to draw a web as shown in Figure 2. Start with the name of a character, a place or a situation in a circle and draw lines radiating out to all the attributes you can associate with the word in the circle—that is, the characteristic qualities of a person or place. Listing them this way helps us to see them more clearly.

You can try this prediction with the same piece you used for the previous prediction exercise. Start by writing down the five question words:

- Who?
- What?
- Where?
- When?
- Why?

Now, next to each of the questions try to write the next

Figure 2   Web diagram

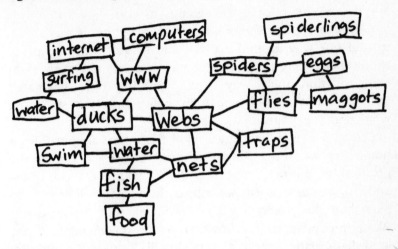

episode of the story. Having done these exercises, you see how you could apply them to other areas of your learning.

Can you imagine?

What you imagine depends on what you know, what you have learnt and what you have experienced. Images came before words, before reasoning, before any other kind of thinking, yet a lot of people now think in words or sounds and have great difficulty putting their imagination to work. Our brains have been programmed so much that we do many things automatically. Our imagination is our automatic pilot: it tells us what to do with our lives, who we are and how to behave.

To help you tap into your imagination, lie on your back and look for 'pictures' in the clouds. Another way to do the same thing is to draw a scribble pattern all over a blank page. Then see what shapes or designs you can find and colour them. Stop and think how you went about this exercise and how you felt while you did it. Albert Einstein believed that genius was made up mostly of imagination. See if you can uncover the genius in you.

Another aspect of this process of imagining is our ability to find our way around a place and to get from one place to another. For example, someone who has lost their sight can still find their way around; and people navigated sailboats on the open ocean by using only the stars, the wind and the patterns of the waves.

Test your own 'navigation' skill when you are away from home: try to draw a map of your house, including the position of all the furniture. Check when you get home and, if necessary, make corrections. We all need to reawaken this ability to use our imagination because our Western education has frowned on it. Imagination of the kind that made you the hero in all kinds of wonderful adventures was, we were told, 'only for children'. But the ability to visualise an object or a situation which is not physically present is directly related to this kind of imagination.

To see how powerful your imagination can be and the effect it can have on your body, just imagine your favourite food in front of you right now. Then check out what's happening in your mouth, your throat and your stomach. The food could just as well be there: your mouth waters, you start swallowing and your stomach starts rumbling. Wouldn't you like to have such a powerful tool to help you learn?

One practical tool for using these skills is called 'mind-mapping'. Tony Buzan invented it and Peter Russell, in his book *The Brain Book*, formulated the following 14 steps:

1 Start in the centre of the page with the topic idea.
2 Work outward in all directions, producing a pattern that reflects your mind's unique habits.
3 Have well-defined clusters and sub-clusters, keeping to 5–7 groupings.

Figure 3   One kind of mind-map

4 Use key words and images.
5 Use colour imagery and 3-D perspectives in your symbols.
6 Print the words, instead of writing them, for more distinct and memorable images.
7 Put the words *on* the lines, not at the end of the lines.
8 Use one word per line. It's more concise.
9 Make the pattern noteworthy, even odd. The mind remembers things that stand out.
10 Use arrows, colours, designs, etc. to show connections.
11 Use personal short-forms, codes for fun and effectiveness.
12 Build at a fast pace. It's more spontaneous and you capture more associations as they occur to you.
13 Be creative and original.
14 Have fun.

Two different kinds of mind-maps are shown in Figures 3 and 4. Now try creating a mind-map of your own with a large sheet of paper and coloured pencils or markers. In

Figure 4 Another kind of mind-map

the middle of the page write the word PAINT. As you think about the word see what directions your mind takes. For each new idea create a branch from the central word.

Some of your thoughts may, in fact, be branches of other branches and this process can go on for quite a long way. It doesn't matter if your thoughts go off at a tangent; just follow this path until it runs out or goes to something completely different.

After a while, start looking for connections. Use arrows, steps and other signs to indicate them. When you feel you've done enough, stop and look at your mind-map. Can you learn anything about how your mind works?

From the mind to the body

Here we come again to images but this time we will see ourselves doing something and doing it really well. This is the way top athletes achieve their goals. They tune in to their bodies and then 'see' themselves going through the actions they need to produce the best possible performance. You can use this method too. To begin getting in touch with your body, try this:

> Walk across the room. Now as you walk back the other way concentrate on the soles of your feet. Think about what is happening to them. How do they move? How do they feel? Now stop walking and remember these things. In your mind, try to recreate the feeling you had in your feet when you were walking. Without moving your feet imagine that you are walking. Can you remember how the bones and muscles moved?

Now choose an activity you are trying to master: playing a musical instrument, reverse parking, your golf swing or how to use a lathe. Go through the movements without actually being there. That is, sit in your chair at home and imagine you are holding a golf club. Think about the position of your feet, your shoulders, your head. Imagine what it would be like to do the action perfectly.

When you have done this, sit down and try to visualise the whole sequence again but this time without moving any part of your body. It won't have any impact if you try it only once, but, like most of the exercises in this chapter, practice will improve your performance. And reflection will help you to transfer the skills to other areas of your learning.

The rhythms of life

Have you stopped lately to think of your sense of hearing? Probably not unless you have a problem with it. For those of us who don't have any difficulties it is something we take very much for granted. Hearing is one part of listening, but not all of it; the other part is engaging the brain in the process.

There are several areas where the importance of listening is obvious: if we are studying music or learning to speak a foreign language. But what about using music to help us in other areas of study? A scientist called Georgi Lozano pioneered a technique for teaching languages by using relaxed deep learning, which has become known as super-learning or accelerated learning. By playing baroque music to students who are fully relaxed and then reading the information to be learned as a background to the music, students learned more words in less time and with less effort than in any other way.

If you want to try this on your own you'll need two tape players. On one you play baroque music until you are in a state of deep relaxation; on the other you play, as background, a recorded list of information you have to learn. This information must be recorded so that it repeats itself three times. When you have heard the information tape three times turn off the music and return to a state of normal awareness. Give yourself a short test to see how much you recall.

Listening to music changes the waves of brain activity. Baroque music shifts brain waves to an alpha state which makes us able to cope better with such tasks as learning a list of new words or anything else that is mechanical or routine.

Think about how you are affected by different types of music: now consider how you can use this information to help you through your day. You may not want lively dance music while you're trying to write an assignment on 'The biodegradable properties of detergents' but wouldn't it be easier to get the household chores done to your favourite tunes?

How about things we need to learn by heart, like formulas, list of dates, names, events? Did you ever chant rhymes or other lists of data when you were young? Do you remember which months have 30 days and which 31? Or do you find yourself muttering: 'thirty days hath September, April, June and November . . .'? After Danny Kaye sang a song about 'the square of the hypotenuse of a right triangle' I never again had trouble remembering Pythagoras' Theorem.

You can use this method by setting to music some of the information you need to learn. Use your favourite tune or one that has a good rhythmical beat. The tunes of old nursery rhymes are easy to use and learn.

Teaching is a good way to learn

We learn much more when we experience things personally, but in one lifetime it simply isn't possible to do this. So we need to learn from teachers, books and our peers, and there are two skills you can develop which will help your learning a lot. The first is to discuss what you learn with another student doing the same subject or with someone who has a good knowledge of the subject. The other, and probably more useful, is to teach someone what you are learning.

Each of these depends on our ability to put ourselves in the other person's place; to be able to think like them; to see their point of view. This is another skill that makes us different from other animals. It also gives us the ability to learn from the experiences and skills of others.

And finally you have yourself

If I am not for myself, who will be for me? But if I am only for myself, what am I?

Hillel

Reflection is a process through which we learn from our own experiences. Instead of just going on and making the same mistakes again and again we go through a process of reflection and analysis. When we learn to go through this process with our successes as well we begin to find that our performance improves quite significantly. We need to become more aware of the things we do, feel, think and say. Here is an exercise that will help you tune in to yourself:

> Choose a task you perform every day: getting dressed; brushing your teeth; washing the dishes. Perform the task in slow motion, watching each and every movement and every part of the task as you do it. Don't think about what you'll do later. Just watch yourself very carefully, taking notice of everything that happens. Don't let yourself 'follow' any other thoughts that come into your head. Pretend they are bubbles and let them float by. When you've finished the task, stop and think about what it was like. What did you learn about yourself? About the way you do things? Did anything surprise you?

In the end, learning is a process. It is also something we all do, whether we are aware of it or not. Every time you do something you have never done before you learn something. How often you do this depends a lot on your personality, your self-esteem, your cultural background and your willingness to go beyond your comfort zone. Learning involves taking chances, and one of the chances we must give ourselves is to take a good hard look at our own behaviour and attitudes. We may not like what we see, but that would be all to the good, because we can then begin to make changes.

Most important of all, though, in this issue of how you learn best, is that the learning process should be enjoyable. It should be a positive experience. We also learn from negative experiences, but we seldom make good use of things we learn in a negative way.

12

What approach does your teacher take?

The authority of those who teach is very often a hindrance to those who wish to learn.

Cicero

TEACHING IS REALLY A MATTER OF LEADERSHIP, AND GOOD TEACHERS—LIKE GOOD managers—don't have to remind their students or subordinates who's boss. This chapter starts with my belief that, as adults, we must take responsibility for our own learning. We should become fully aware of our own preferred learning style, our personality type, our family and social obligations and our work or career commitments. Once we have done that we can take charge of our learning and give it our best shot.

School education, in the main, operates on the 'jug and mugs' system: the teacher is a jug, full of knowledge, and the children are mugs, to be filled. This doesn't work with adults. Our 'mugs' already have something in them. Another way of describing what happens with children is the 'blank slate' theory. Their minds are blank slates on which the teacher will 'write' a lot of knowledge. Think for a minute about all the things you already have written on your 'slate'.

There are several different kinds of teachers: the one who encourages the students to voice their own views and feelings; the one who is definitely in charge all the time; and the teacher who is the group leader just because of their position. For easy identification let's give each of them a name: we'll call the first the Facilitator, the second the Lion-tamer and the third the Prince(ss) Regent.

The Facilitator

The teacher who has consciously decided on this role is the best kind. He or she understands that students come with a whole lot of emotional and mental baggage; that adult students have cultural and religious beliefs and perceptions that will influence the way they understand and accept information; that students have various other commitments; that mature-age students are usually highly motivated and have choices, of which study is only one. The good facilitator:

- lets students express their feelings and their views
- lets students learn from one another
- treats—and speaks to—students as adults
- can admit to errors or gaps in their own knowledge
- can resolve conflict between students
- makes fair and unbiased decisions
- has a sound knowledge of the subject and/or access to a variety of resources
- works individually with students to bring out the best in them.

Coping with the Facilitators shouldn't pose too many problems. They eventually get around to most of the students' learning needs. However, when they are very familiar with their subject it is sometimes difficult for them to understand how complex it seems to the students. This is when it becomes important for students to ask questions.

Fortunately, the Facilitators are usually happy to answer them.

Of course this kind of teacher doesn't suit everyone. Many of us have a different view of what teaching and learning are about. There are a couple of reasons for this. One is the 'empty slate' theory I mentioned before. We have been taught that the teacher is the person with the knowledge and that if we pay attention and do as we're told we'll learn. When the Facilitator asks for student participation in a discussion, three things happen to these students:

1 They don't accept their peers as having any worthwhile knowledge to share—so they don't listen.
2 They don't believe they have anything to contribute—so they don't talk.
3 Worst of all—they stop thinking when other students are talking.

Another reason mature students have difficulties with the Facilitator is that they don't know how to decide what they need to learn. Basically, what these students want is the Lion-tamer.

The Lion-tamer

Many Lion-tamers are teachers who have 'graduated' from school to adult education. They believe in 'discipline' and they hand out lists of 'objectives'. They have their own plan either because they are worried about covering everything in the syllabus or because they see some things as important or right.

A Lion-tamer's presentation is often fairly rigid and narrowly focused, and students' comments and questions tend to be ignored or put down. It could go something like this:

(a) 'You will learn Pythagoras' Theorem.' The teacher then writes the theorem on the board, explains the working and asks if everyone understands that. There won't, however, be time to say you didn't understand because the teacher goes straight on to the next objective.

(b) 'You will learn twenty new words' (in a foreign language class). The teacher then hands out copies of a list of words with their English equivalents, gives two or three examples of how these are used in sentences, asks one or two students to give examples, then asks the class to write sentences using the words.

(c) 'You will learn how to paint a picture of a tree.' The teacher then shows pictures of several different types of trees, talks about techniques and then gets students to draw trees which must look like the ones shown.

The Lion-tamers' main characteristics are a reluctance to give up the position of authority, and a tendency to dismiss as unimportant any questions they can't answer. They also expect the group's attention to remain focused on them. If you're stuck with a teacher like this and you don't like it, there are several courses of action you can take:

• Try to get a transfer to another class—but check out the teacher of that class before you ask for this!

• Get the assessment scheme (from the teacher) and the curriculum outline (from the library) and become a self-directed learner.

• Team up with one or two other students who feel the way you do and form your own study group.

If you choose either of the last two alternatives, make sure you still attend classes. Use the class lesson to pick up information about assessment criteria and likely exam questions. After all, failing the course won't affect the teacher, and attendance is usually one of the requirements.

The Prince(ss) Regent

This is the teacher who is still wondering how they got

there. They may be new to teaching and if that's the case, be kind to them and help them learn, because to be a good teacher you need to learn from your students. Most of all, try to be gentle. Confrontation is the last thing this teacher needs: they probably wouldn't be able to cope with it. They know that authority goes with their job but because of their insecurity they refer queries to head teachers or other superiors and they hide behind institutional rules when students challenge them.

If you explain your learning needs clearly and carefully to this teacher, they will most likely do their best to help you. Their main problem is usually a lack of experience. They don't give well-defined starting-points for group discussions; they're afraid of silence so they don't give students time to think; they ask questions that are too simple and they hover when students are working independently or in small groups. They can also give such dogmatic replies to questions that discussion comes to an abrupt end. You can deal with (and help) this teacher by:

- asking questions to help them focus on the level and point the students need to start from
- discussing your need for thinking time and silence— make encouraging suggestions to help the teacher accept this.

Classes are really groups and groups exist because their members have a common goal. It isn't enough for you to know what you want from the group—you should also think what you can contribute to the group. Good adult educators give students the opportunity to do this. They try to discover, as early in the course as possible, what expertise the student group has. Don't feel that a teacher who does this is 'copping out'. The best kind of teaching and learning is interactive: there must be input from students as well as from the teacher.

Everyone, students and teacher, must keep an open

mind. Having always dealt with adults I'm happy to admit that I learn constantly from my students. Quite often I use anecdotes they've told me to illustrate a point for another class. When I want them to think about something I turn it into a class discussion: they are just as likely to listen to their peers' opinions as to any theories I might produce. On the other hand, I don't want any student to feel that they must believe the same things I do.

Group leaders

The obvious leader in the classroom is the teacher, but groups usually have two leaders. If this isn't obvious from the beginning it will certainly be apparent by the third meeting. This alternate leader usually has a considerable amount of influence and if it's used in a positive way it can help to overcome some of the teacher's shortcomings.

In the language of group communication the teacher is the formal leader and the student leader is the informal leader. The formal leader is responsible for 'product', that is, what everyone does, the work they produce or, in this case, what they learn. The informal leader is responsible for 'process'—how everyone feels about the work, the place and each other. But don't leave it all up to the leaders. You'll get what you give, and remember, groups, like people, have good days and bad days.

13

Lectures and listening

WE SPEND ALMOST HALF OUR WAKING HOURS listening and yet for most of us this is our least developed skill in the communication process. Listening is hard work; it's not just hearing sounds. It's done with the eyes, touch, mind, heart and imagination as well as with the ears. Hearing is an involuntary action. If there is sound near us we will hear it. Afterwards we may or may not recall having heard it. If we are listening we will remember, perhaps not everything, but quite a substantial part. A good listener is an active listener.

Too often we have fixed ideas that get in the way of a message someone is trying to send us. When we hear a word we don't like (it could be anything—spinach, abortion, work) we are immediately distracted by our views about it and stop paying attention. Or we think we know what the speaker is about to say because their subject is something we know about, so we stop listening and start thinking about what we will say. It is impossible to give the speaker your full attention while you are trying to plan your next speech.

Of course, there are all sorts of other barriers to listening, such as outside interference—other people talking, a radio playing loudly, traffic noise, machinery and movement in the background. You can probably think of at least one or two others. It takes practice, but you can learn to ignore all these and pay careful attention to the speaker.

Good listening starts with concentrating, goes on with involvement and requires lots of feedback. Don't stop listening because the subject matter seems difficult or boring. If it's difficult, try asking the speaker to clarify any points you have trouble with. In a lecture this is difficult—sometimes even impossible—but you can do it in tutorials and you should certainly be able to do it in ordinary classes. Some lecturers make unfair assumptions about what students should already know.

If you have this problem with a particular lecturer, talk to some of your fellow students. Perhaps you could go as a (small) group and explain your problem to the lecturer—he or she may not be aware of it. This problem sometimes occurs with a lecturer who has a different language background. No matter how good their English is, differences in their sentence construction can cause difficulty if you don't listen carefully.

Attention

Attentiveness is the first and most important element of good listening. Unless you give the process your full attention you are not really listening. Attentive listening is indicated by such things as posture and gestures. We all know that posture tells us someone is in a hurry to leave. They are half turned away from you when you are still speaking to them, ready to move away at the first pause. You know they aren't really listening but you go on speaking. To get their full attention, ask them a question and wait for the reply. Better yet, if you feel the conversation is important, stop talking and suggest a meeting at a more convenient time. When you are the listener, let the other person know that you are in a hurry and, if the matter is important, arrange to spend time together when it is more convenient for both of you.

Eye contact is another way to show that you are listening, and to tell whether the other person is listening to you. In lectures this is difficult because when you take notes your head is down. Try to look up at the lecturer as often as you can, to let them know that you are still interested: it does wonders for the lecturer's morale. The lecturer, on the other hand, may have to keep looking at his or her notes, but should also look around the room at the students.

One other skill we need, which comes with practice, is the ability to 'shut out' all distractions. Don't let your mind wander. When you find yourself thinking of something else—an assignment that's due, tomorrow evening's outing, whatever—let the thought go, and bring your mind back to the lecture or discussion.

Comprehending

To follow what is being said you need skills in concentrating, short-term and long-term memory, questioning, and attentiveness. You also need some understanding of the material being presented. To make this easier try reading something of the topic before class. If you don't know what it will be about, find out from the teacher or a student. Most teachers hand out reading lists and a brief course outline at the beginning. If they don't you should ask. You may have to ask each week, at the end of the lesson, what the next lesson will cover. You may also have to explain to the teacher that you want to be prepared!

Learn to ask questions that will get the information you need. Open questions are those which demand more than a 'yes' or 'no' response. Questions that begin with what, where, when, how and why get more informative replies than those that begin with do, can or are. This doesn't mean that you always have to ask open questions. Sometimes, when you want to check if you have the right information or not, you can ask a closed question. If the answer is not the one you expected, ask an open question to get more information.

Action and reflection

Another important part of the listening process is acting on what we have heard and reflecting on it. You have to decide that you want to listen. Once you've decided that, you must pay attention and accept the responsibility of doing your fair share in the communication process.

You need to think about what is being said, to ask someone to repeat points you don't quite understand or say them in a different way to make them clear. This takes concentration as well as an effort to see the speaker's point of view. Try to put yourself in their place: does it then become easier to understand them?

Open-mindedness is not the easiest thing to achieve, but it is worth the effort. It means we gain much more from our interactions with other people, we listen more carefully, understand better what is being said, and give unbiased responses. In terms of better communication it pays to be open-minded.

Some dangers

Something that gets in the way of our listening is jumping ahead, when we think we know what the other person is going to say. This is dangerous because we stop listening and start thinking about what we are going to say when the other person stops speaking. We also think about other things while someone else is speaking because we can think five or six times faster than we speak.

Trying to take notes while we listen also endangers the listening process, mainly because we tend to ignore all the other means of communication we usually tune in to, like posture, gestures and tone of voice. This is why it's so important to look up as often as possible at the lecturer when you're taking notes.

Selfconsciousness also stops us from listening. Sometimes we are more concerned about what others think of us than we are with what they are saying so we don't give them our full attention. Or we start dreaming, thinking we are listening, but suddenly finding that the other person has stopped, and is waiting expectantly. Obviously they expect a response and you can't remember what they said.

Anxiety about the message we hear is another distraction. Either the situation is stressful or the message is somehow problematical. Because you feel anxious the message becomes distorted, you think you hear something the other person isn't really saying, react to what you think you heard—and communication breaks down.

During a discussion on euthanasia, Roz was convinced that Barry's point of view would be completely opposite to her own. As the conversation became more heated Roz began to sound very defensive in her attempt to persuade the group to her way of thinking. Barry was saying much the same; he had merely added one proviso that Roz hadn't mentioned. Even the rest of the group couldn't convince her that Barry shared her point of view. She was totally convinced that her view differed from Barry's.

Sometimes you hear only what you expect to hear; you have some preconceived idea of what you will hear and this is all you do hear. Quite often what we expect to hear is nothing like what the speaker is saying, but because we are so good at fooling ourselves, we believe what we think we heard.

Being judgmental is also a block to good listening. If you are making judgments about the speaker and the material they present you won't really understand what is being said. It takes practice to listen with an open mind, to take in carefully what is being said, and reserve judgment for later.

Speakers

Long speeches do tend to become boring, that's why it's so hard to sit through university lectures without falling asleep. Which led some bright (anonymous) student to write on a desk:

> Now I lay me back to sleep,
> The speaker's dull, the subject's deep,
> If he should stop before I wake,
> Give me a nudge for goodness' sake.

It would seem that the only reason for lecturing at university is that it's the cheapest way to give information to a lot of students at once. It certainly isn't the ideal way to learn anything, but universities have been teaching in this way for about 400 years, and that's probably the way it will stay. We all learn to put up with it. What we have to learn is how to learn the material in better ways. There are tutorial groups for most subjects, usually conducted as small group discussions. For these you will be expected to prepare material, and to discuss the subject in depth, usually with a tutor who is not the lecturer.

Small group discussions

Thorough preparation is important because it gives you a clearer idea of what you want to discuss and you'll remember the discussion more clearly. A group that meets regularly, like a tutorial group, develops some cohesion and understanding of one another. This means that people in the group begin to recognise each other's opinions, views and ways of expressing themselves. Then we need to learn to distinguish information from opinion. There is little point in letting someone's opinions upset you: they are, after all, entitled to hold those opinions, just as you are entitled to yours. It takes some practice not to become upset by others' opinions, but it's worth the effort; it will certainly make you a better student.

As the group grows and develops we need to sharpen our listening skills. We need to listen on another level and notice subtle signals like a lift of the eyebrow, a frown, a wave of the hand. These add to the meaning of the words we use and noticing them is part of good listening.

When listening to a presentation by a fellow student try not to let yourself be distracted by such things as the speaker's appearance, strange mannerisms or speech peculiarities. Let the words sink in before you respond. Allowing a few seconds silence at the end of someone else's speech suggests that you are considering your reply carefully. Giving feedback, to show that you have understood, gives you time to think again about what has been said. Your next response will then be better thought out, and probably better expressed. The following may be useful:

T I L E

Tune in   Inquire   Listen   Evaluate

Tune in: Be ready to listen from the beginning.

Inquire: Think of questions you either need to ask or look for answers to during the talk. Sometimes you can ask questions during the talk, other times you may need to wait until the speaker has finished.

Listen: Here we mean listen actively. Be aware of other levels of communication such as the non-verbal signals, the tone of voice, the rate of speaking, the facial expressions of the speaker and so on.

Evaluate: Make a preliminary decision, as the person is speaking, about whether you agree with what's being said. This will help you to listen more carefully.

And remember to take notes—brief ones! Write down key words or short phrases to remind yourself of the points made.

14

Resources, resources, resources

RESOURCES COME IN A VARIETY OF SHAPES and sizes. Any person or thing that gives you the information you need is a resource. Some of us ask people we think will know; some of us head straight for the library. But have you ever stopped to think of any other resources? Think about the information you could get from the following:

- government departments: e.g. the Bureau of Statistics, Housing, Health, Women's Issues
- large corporations: e.g. banks, mining companies, pharmaceutical manufacturers
- service clubs: e.g. Rotary, Lions, St John's Ambulance
- amateur societies: e.g. historical societies, photographic and other hobby clubs
- professional people: e.g. doctors, dentists, solicitors.

Most organisations, societies and clubs publish newsletters or journals which they are happy to share with people like you and me, and these are listed in the phonebook.

Which books you have to buy depends on the course you choose, but at the very least you'll need a dictionary and a thesaurus.

Choosing a dictionary

Dictionaries are not all the same, and they don't stay the same. Only dictionaries of dead languages—such as Latin—stay the same. Any living, spoken language changes and develops continually, so it's no good buying an old dictionary unless you're planning to make your writing sound old-fashioned (or studying linguistics). If English is your first (or only) language you still need a good dictionary—and a very up-to-date one at that—because learning new ideas and new information means learning new words. To use these new words correctly you have to understand their meanings, and to use them in your written work you have to know how to spell them correctly.

Because good dictionaries are not cheap, choose carefully. If you have an old one, use it for a while and think carefully about its replacement. One of the best general dictionaries to come out in recent years is the Collin's Co-Build. Besides the meanings of words it gives examples of how to use them in idiomatic expressions and phrases.

Then, depending on your subject, you also need a small specialised dictionary. Collins puts out a range in small format for subjects ranging from anthropology to zoology and everything in between. But don't go rushing out to buy one for every subject you enrol in. You'll get the most use out of a dictionary like this when you study a subject in depth. At the beginning you should find everything you need in the general dictionary.

Thesaurus

This lovely word comes from the Greek word for treasure and Roget compiled the best. Roget (pronounced Roh-jay) was a doctor whose Thesaurus of Synonyms and Antonyms has been in use since 1852. My edition, published in 1972, has been enlarged and revised by two successive members of the Roget family, and is the most often used book in my collection. It is absolutely vital because it can enlarge your vocabulary like no other single reference. A dictionary gives you just the meaning of a word, but Roget gives you all the possible variations of the way to say something and all the opposite meanings as well.

At first you may be tempted to look up words and use the longest or most impressive-looking one you find. Be careful, though. When you find a word that looks, sounds or feels right, check the dictionary. You may find that the current meaning of the word has changed since your thesaurus edition was published. Usually, however, you'll find a word that you know but hadn't thought of. When you find yourself using the same few adjectives such as great, nice and beautiful all the time, try the thesaurus for some alternatives.

The book is divided into two sections: first you look up the word you have in mind in the back section. Let's look up 'nice'. We find it in the alphabetical listing like this:

nice—
      savory 394
      discriminative 465
      exact 494
      good 648
      pleasing 829
      fastidious 868
      honourable 939
—ear 418
—hand 700
—perception 465
—point 704

The numbers are not page numbers but entry numbers. Each entry in the front half of the book is divided into sections with abbreviations: N for nouns, V for verbs, Adj.

for adjectives and Adv. for adverbs. Don't worry too much if you haven't learnt the difference between a noun and a verb. Just go through the lists until you find the word you started with; in this case, 'nice'.

Most of us use 'nice' when we want to talk about 'good', so we'll look up the entry 648. Next to the number is the word 'goodness' and a list of words such as 'excellence, merit, virtue, value'. That's not what we want. A little further along we find 'V. be beneficial, do good, profit'. Not quite what we want either. The next section is Adj. and starts with 'harmless, beneficial, valuable' and, further along, our original 'nice'. This, then, is the section we need. Try out some of the words in your own sentences, and choose one that works better than 'nice'.

Encyclopedias

A good set, besides being very costly, is really only as good as its annual updates. If you don't already own a set don't go rushing out to buy one. Some of their information on contemporary subjects, discoveries, and so on, has become out of date. Another important point about encyclopedias is that they are biased: some person or people had to decide what to include and what to leave out.

And don't think that because something's in the encyclopedia it must be correct, either. One I looked at tells me that 99 per cent of all US citizens are literate and yet several more authoritative sources state that only about 65 per cent of them are literate.

Encyclopedias are fine as a first source of reference. They usually give you very basic facts about your subject and most of them also suggest other, associated topics. When you have half an hour to spare, browse through the reference books in your library so that the next time you need a certain piece of information you'll know where to look.

Libraries

Don't be afraid of the library. Think of it as a treasure house, something like an Egyptian tomb. There is wealth untold within but you need to find your way. A very useful book is *Mastering the Maze* by Christine Fogg, published jointly by the Australian Centre for Independent Journalism and the University of Technology, Sydney, in 1994. It tells you about all the things you'll find in the library, as well as special libraries, special collections and government publications.

When you go into any library for the first time ask at the information desk for help. Most libraries have pamphlets, brochures or booklets explaining their services, collections and facilities, the borrowing rights you are entitled to, and how to use all these. Most Australian libraries use the Dewey cataloguing system. Books are grouped together according to subject and then, within these groups, alphabetically by author surname.

Collections

Different libraries specialise in different areas. In Sydney the public libraries each have a different main collection. They still have books on other topics, but they have more on their special subject. For example, one municipality specialises in automotive books and holds all kinds of car manuals, even those that are now out of print, for cars we no longer see on the roads.

University libraries have good collections on subjects they specialise in. No university teaches every possible subject. Universities with more than one campus keep different subjects in separate buildings on different campuses.

Catalogues

These are put on cards or on computer. Don't be afraid of the computers. Ask a librarian to show you how to use them. Learn to use them; you can't damage them. The worst that can happen is that you'll get back to the blank screen with only the DOS prompt: C>. Even some academic staff don't know how to use the library properly so don't feel embarrassed if you need to ask for help. Practise using the catalogues whenever you can. Practice makes you efficient and fast. Stay focused: don't be tempted to go off on a tangent. Catalogues are not for browsing, so use them only if you know exactly what you need.

To start a search you need at least one of the following:

- author's name
- book title
- subject heading.

When you have more than one of these the computer will let you combine them to narrow your search and speed it up. Once you find the book—or other item—the computer will tell you the Dewey or catalogue number and whether the book is on the shelf or on loan to another borrower, but it isn't always right. Sometimes the book is being used by someone in the library; it may have been mis-shelved; or it may have been damaged and is being repaired.

If the book you want is not available don't wait around for it. Even if the library sends out a recall notice there is no guarantee that the other person will return the item immediately. There are always alternative sources of information. Try journal articles as well as other books.

Remember also that most things that are available on computer are also available in print. So, until you learn how to use the computer confidently and efficiently, consult the print versions when you have a deadline.

Computers

Apart from the computer catalogues most academic libraries also have facilities for students to use computers for word processing and research, and some will give you access to Internet. Ask about these, find brochures about them and make use of them.

Staff

Librarians are not just people who put books back on shelves. They are the ones with the information about information. Good librarians not only know what they have in their own libraries, they also know where to find the things they don't have, and have access to them. They have publications available at the information desk for different levels of students about different topic areas. If you don't understand something, ask at the Information Desk. Library staff in large academic libraries are divided into liaison teams. In addition, individual librarians are attached to different faculties. Their function is to help students and staff. They also order new books, develop the collection, pass on things which come in and may be of use in research, and make students and staff aware of the resources available. Staff on the information desk should be able to deal with most queries. When things get more complex you may have to consult the liaison person.

Closed reserve

This system operates in TAFE and university libraries: books in heavy demand are shelved in a different part of the library and are available for only 2 or 3 hours at a time. If the books the lecturer told you to use are not available, either because they're out on loan or because the lecturer didn't notify the library in time, there are other avenues. One of these is called 'serials'. In library terms serials are publications that arrive regularly—for example, daily news-papers, fortnightly newsletters, monthly journals, annual directories and yearbooks.

Some libraries shelve their serials among the books, others shelve them separately. Find out what happens to them in the library you will be using most often. Many journal articles are now available on CD-ROM so learn how to use this to gain access to this usually very up-to-date information.

Interlibrary loans

These are available to you at your local public library but not at most academic libraries: it would be far too costly. However, some universities have reciprocal borrowing rights. Check this out with the staff at your own university. To take advantage of this you need a printout of your borrower's record to show the other library that you don't have any overdue borrowings. Don't be afraid to use the library at a university, even if you aren't an enrolled student. You are free to walk in, look around, use the catalogue, read, study, use the photocopiers—you always have to pay for the copies anyway—and if you can't find something you want, ask the staff. Mastering the system in one library helps you to find your way around others.

Self-directed learning

This sounds as if the teachers are opting out of their responsibility for teaching, but students gain a great deal when they take responsibility for their own learning. The main point of this book is to give you ideas and information which will help you become a better, self-directed learner. As a rule adults are more self-directed than school-leavers. We have a better idea of what we want even if we don't always know how to get it. Also, having been out in the big world we know why we want it. Our motivation is high and so are our expectations. What we are usually short on—and this isn't really a bad thing—is the patience to put up with what we see as waffle.

Remember, 'self-directed' means that you don't wait for the teacher to tell you every move to make. You take on the responsibility of finding material, doing extra reading rather than the bare minimum, forming study groups with fellow students and generally taking charge of your own education within the framework of the class program.

15

Reading and note-taking

BECAUSE THIS IS THE BASIS OF EVERY PIECE of work you do, it's important to develop good note-taking habits from the start. There are two different kinds of notes: those you make from your reading and research and those you take in lectures.

Lecture notes

We'll start with the lecture notes because they usually come first in the scheme of things. You go along to the lecture, listen to the teacher's pearls of wisdom, along with the jokes, anecdotes and other pieces of extra information which a good lecturer puts in to lighten the subject. Don't feel that you have to write down every word the lecturer utters. Learn to listen for key words and important information on the subject. To do this properly you should do some preparation before you go to the lecture.

Find out what the lecture will be about: at least the topic, but more if possible, to get a good idea of what information is important or not. Do some preliminary reading to familiarise yourself with the topic. Make sure you have all the right equipment: several pens or pencils—you

112

don't want to be stuck with a pen that doesn't write or a pencil with a broken point—a pad of paper and a clipboard.

Then, get to the lecture early or at least on time. There are two reasons for this: you'll have a better chance of getting a seat near the front with all the other (more experienced) mature students, and you'll be there to hear the lecturer's introduction.

A good lecturer organises the lecture this way:

1   Tell them what you're going to tell them.
2   Tell them.
3   Tell them what you've told them.

The introduction and the conclusion are important. A good introduction tunes your mind to the subject and makes your note-taking easier and more relevant. Listening to the conclusion is also important because the points that are repeated or stressed in this part of the lecture often come up in quizzes, tests and exams.

Once you get into the lecture room—or perhaps even before—write the date, the name of the lecturer and the subject at the top of the page and number the pages as you go: it's always the pages I don't number that I drop and never seem able to get back in the right order.

Taking notes in lectures doesn't have to be confined to writing down the words the lecturer says. If you are a highly visual person—have you read Chapter 2?—you might draw a picture or a mind-map or some other graphic description of the subject matter. But don't try this just for fun, especially not in an important lecture that you cannot attend again.

It is most important that you can read your notes again and make sense of them, even when you come back to them several weeks later. On the other hand, if you are an audio person you may prefer to tape-record the lecture. This, however, needs permission from the lecturer. If you do use a tape recorder, sit in the front, use a sensitive microphone and edit as you go. To do this instant editing you must learn to listen carefully. Chapter 13 tells you more about this important skill.

An exercise that can help you with your note-taking skills for lectures is to watch and make notes on a documentary on television. Then use your notes to write a piece on the documentary's main theme and treatment. You could do the same with a radio program.

For more about what to do with your lecture notes read Chapter 16 on revision, Chapter 17 on essay writing and Chapter 19 on exams.

Research and reading

The notes you take while doing research are the foundation on which you build every piece of writing you hand in for assessment. With the huge amount of information available in most libraries these days it is so tempting to photocopy every possible thing we find and then take home a stack of these pages. One alternative is unthinkable: to take home a huge stack of books. The other alternative is to make time to read and take notes in the library. And there is a good reason for making notes the 'old-fashioned' way, with paper and pencil: it helps you to put things into your own words as you read.

If you simply photocopy what you think are the right pages and take them home you risk finding that you should have done at least two or three more pages, or a different chapter. The other problem a lot of my students have with photocopies is that they forget to photocopy or write down the bibliography details. Sometimes the name of the book appears at the top of the page, but more often it doesn't, and when you go back you can't remember which book the section came from.

Getting it done

You've done a library search, found seven books, three journal articles and a video on the topic, and put them on the table. When you sit down the top of the stack is at eye level and your mind goes blank. Go back to your essay topic. Let's say it's the mating habits of the boggle-eyed blackfish. You found only one small booklet on this particular fish (all the other books are more general) and that was written for people who have a fish tank at home. Your essay is for a biology class and needs more detail. Don't ignore the booklet: it may have something you can use, but don't spend more than a minute or two on it. If it has a contents list at the front, check the headings. There may be a chapter or section on mating habits. If this is more than two or three pages look in the index (if there is one) for related words. For example, you may find 'fertilisation', 'eggs', 'gestation' or 'spawning', and perhaps one of these entries leads you to a useful paragraph. Read it and, before you make any notes about it, write the name of the author, the book title, the place of publication, the publisher and the year of publication at the top of your page. Then write the page number of the entry in the left margin.

Now read the paragraph/s and briefly note, in your own words, what you have just learned. When you read something you think is so well-written that you don't want to change it, write it down word for word, but remember that you must use quotation marks ('. . .').

Even when a book is the prescribed text for your course, don't feel that you have to read it from cover to cover as you would with a novel. Before you start any research for a written assignment, read Chapter 17 and learn how to structure your essay or report to make the research faster and more efficient. Go back to Chapter 16, too, to see what kind of notes you need to revise efficiently for tests and exams.

16

Revision and thinking

REVISION AND THINKING GO TOGETHER LIKE bread and cheese: you can separate them but the combination is a sandwich. To do good revision you need to think. Exercise your brain—make it work. But don't wait until the test or exam is about to happen. Do some revision every week. It takes time but you knew when you started that you would have to give up a lot of time to get through the course. And as someone once said, life wasn't meant to be easy.

When to revise

At the end of a lesson or lecture take 4–5 minutes to read through the notes you made. Add anything you may have missed. Once you get into the habit of doing this it doesn't seem to take much time and you can always meet the rest of the group in the canteen or the pub a few minutes later.

In the evening spend another 5 minutes reading through the notes once more. Use a highlight pen or underline key words and phrases. Draw a diagram or a picture of some of the information, do a mind-map of some kind. This process helps you put the information into a form you can remember more easily. When you've done all this—it shouldn't take more than 10–15 minutes—put the notes in a file or a box with your other notes for the same subject.

At the end of the week take out the file and skim through it for about half an hour. Don't agonise over anything. Just relax and read through your notes to refresh your memory. If, while you're reading, you get a feeling of surprise—'I had forgotten that'—underline or highlight that point and go on reading. Check the mind-maps and other visual representations you made, perhaps adding some more details, then put it all away.

Two or three days before a test spend 2–3 hours reading and revising. For more about what to do with this time, look at the following section of this chapter on revision.

The evening before the test read through your notes one more time and then get an early night. Don't panic. Don't try to cram at the last minute and don't discuss the test with other—probably nervous—students. Your biggest advantage is a feeling of confidence with a light touch of nerves. And after the test don't discuss your answers with other students either. There is absolutely no benefit in worrying about your result.

How to revise

To understand the best way for you to revise you need to do two things: find out what sort of learner you are (Chapter 2) and which ways you learn best (Chapter 11).

Dominic learnt best when he illustrated his work: a combination of words and pictures helped him recall the material. For each topic he had to learn he made a small poster and put them all up on the walls of his room. As he lay in bed, before going to sleep, he flashed a torch on these posters at random and tried to recall, in the instant before he could see it, what he would find there. By the time the exam came round he knew them all. After the exam he was asked how he felt. He said he felt as though he'd cheated: 'It was so easy. All I had to do was "look" at the posters.' Would you feel as though you'd been cheating?

Study can be this easy if we start looking at all the other ways of learning. In Chapter 11 you read about using all your senses and some ways of learning. If you found ways that suited you best right from the start then you should have the right sort of 'notes' for your revision. Use your preferred way to learn. It may seem you are 'wasting time' because it will probably be easy for you to learn this way. And haven't we all been taught that anything worthwhile is difficult, requires effort, even pain? It's not true!

One of the best tools I know for revision is a kind of mind-map. We've already talked about these and they are useful in several ways. As a revision tool I don't know anything that works better. You start preparing for a test or an exam by looking at past papers and any notes you've made of clues from the teacher about what will be in the test. Every teacher gives these clues—some do it quite openly: 'There will be a question on this topic'; others do it without realising. They say something like 'This is really important' or 'Listen carefully' or 'Are you sure you understand all this?' Teachers really don't want you to fail unless you have not handed in work, been absent too often from class, or had a major clash with them. So they give out signals that will help you to narrow down your pre-test studies to a manageable amount.

Now, having looked at these notes and past papers, choose one topic you feel you should review. Don't, for the moment, open your notes on this topic. Start with a blank sheet of paper. Write the topic heading in the middle of the page. Now write—or draw—everything you can think of about the topic. Don't spend more than 10 minutes on this but don't waste time either. If you run out of things to write and you just can't think of anything else within 30–40 seconds, stop.

Now, open your book, file or whatever you have for the topic. Go through the notes, ticking off every item on the mind-map. At the end of this step any item that hasn't been ticked needs some thorough revision; everything that has been ticked is stored in your long-term memory. Just as you were able to recall these things today for your revision, you'll be able to recall them in the exam. By the time I learned this technique I had only one more exam to write. It worked so well that I now teach all my students to use it for revision for tests and exams. It's the only way I know to find the gaps in your knowledge.

Of course it isn't always as easy as I make it sound. We have other important things that crop up in our lives— usually unexpectedly—and for one reason or another we let the studies slide for a week or two. Then, when we get back to them, we find that we have fallen behind and it becomes more and more difficult to catch up. If this happens, and you can't get an extension on an assignment, or the exam is coming up very soon, you still have one or two options.

One is to take a day or two of your holidays and put in a concerted effort. The other is the one I know many students take and I wish they wouldn't: they drop out of the course and never come back. Dropping out *is* a viable option, but what I say to those few students who tell me they intend to drop out is that they should leave the door open. Don't just disappear, have a fail mark recorded against your name and never come back because you're too embarrassed. Talk to the student counsellor. If they can't help, at least they can tell you how to withdraw from the class and keep open the option of trying again next semester or next year. There is no shame attached to this. Adults do have different priorities at different times of their lives, and sometimes we do make mistakes about the timing of events.

PART 4

Showing what you've learned

17

Essays and reports

MOST MATURE-AGE STUDENTS ARE AFRAID they won't be very good at written assignments. Like any other skill, good factual writing can be learned. The kind of writing you'll have to do depends on several factors:

- your college or university
- the individual teacher of your subject
- the type of assignment.

Each of these will affect not only what you write but where you get your information, how you write it and how you present your finished work for marking. Beginning with the kind of writing you'd expect to do in informal classes we'll work through the different formats up to an undergraduate degree at university.

Notes

To help you remember what you've learned in class, take notes. That doesn't mean writing down every word the teacher says; just jot down key words. Don't write full sentences. Develop your own code. Use diagrams and sketches. Try flowcharts. Use coloured pencils and highlight pens. At the end of the lesson or the day, spend 5–6 minutes reading through these notes. Add anything you remember but haven't noted and then file them with other notes for the same subject. If the subject is a practical one, like pottery or cooking, keep a small notebook with you always for noting down ideas when they occur to you.

Paragraphs

In a class test or an exam you may be asked to write a paragraph on a particular topic. In practical terms this means that you will write between four and eight sentences, each containing one piece of information on the topic. You should be able to judge, more or less, from the number of marks the question carries, how many points you need to make. If the question is worth five marks you'll need to write at least five sentences, each with one correct piece of information, to get those marks. If you can think of a sixth point quickly, put it in, but don't worry if you can't. In an exam you seldom have time for this extra thinking.

Getting the structure of a paragraph is very much like the structuring of an essay. Ask yourself: what, where, when, who, why and how. You might have more than one answer to one of these and none for another. That's all right—be flexible. Those questions are there to get you started. Here is an example paragraph:

> Writing a paragraph is quite simple. First make a list, on a spare sheet of paper, of the points you will address. Next put them into a logical sequence, in their order of occurrence or importance, for example. Then write a sentence for each point: this is your first draft. Now read this through, making corrections to grammar, spelling and general flow. Last, write a closing sentence to restate your topic sentence in a slightly different form. You see, it's not really difficult to write a paragraph.

Topic sentences for paragraphs quite often look as though they need to continue with the word 'because' but you should strongly resist the temptation to do this. Try writing some paragraphs of your own. To start you off here are some topic sentences.

- Children should be taught to help with the household chores.
- Holidays are good for the soul.
- Everyone should have a goal.

Now think up one or two topic sentences of your own.

Book reviews

Depending, again, on the subject you are studying, book reviews vary. Here is a general outline for writing one:

Introduction

Name the title and author and write just a few sentences about the theme of the story, the author, and whether you liked it or not. Whatever the order of your sentences in your introduction, write a paragraph about each, in the same order.

Body

- *Theme* Explain what the writer wants to tell you: what is the meaning of the story?
- *Plot* In a few lines tell the main events of the story.
- *Story* Tell the story in one paragraph.
- *Main character* Describe the personality and physical features.
- *Other characters* Describe as many and as fully as possible.

Conclusion

Tell the reader whether you recommend it or not. Repeat the theme in one or two sentences. This involves rewriting the introduction in different words and adding your recommendation.

Use this plan thoughtfully. For example, if you're studying English literature this will be the form you'll use but you'll be expected to write more than 'a few lines', 'one paragraph' or 'one or two sentences'. On the other hand, if you are reviewing a textbook you won't need to write anything about theme, plot or story, but you'll need to put in headings such as 'theories', 'research', 'recommendations' and 'possible applications'. You'll also have to write something about the book's layout of material and whether or not you found the information easy to understand and useful.

Essays

There aren't any secrets to writing good essays or reports, but there are some rules.

Rule 1: Define your topic

Read the essay question carefully. Make sure you really understand what the assignment is about. Avoid the trap John fell into. He was given an assignment to describe and discuss French Colonial Art by presenting an artist of the period (length: 1000 words). He looked up the French Colonial period and found so much information about it that he didn't look at one particular artist. He wrote a 2000-word general report on the period and failed.

Here is a list of key words used in essay questions, together with definitions and descriptions of what they are asking you to do.

Analyse: Break up the subject into its main ideas. Examine them systematically, then try to describe the relationship between them.

Compare: Look for characteristics that resemble each other. Emphasise similarities but also mention differences.

Contrast: Stress the differences of things, qualities or problems.

Criticise: Analyse as fully as possible the merit or truth of the facts or views mentioned, discussing their limitations and good points.

Define: Give precise meanings, with a few key details. A contrast may be useful here.

Describe: Recount, characterise, sketch or relate in sequence or story form.

Diagram: Give a drawing, chart, plan or some other graphic form of answer. Label your diagram and, if appropriate, add a brief caption (explanation).

Discuss: Analyse carefully, give reasons for and against, and give full details.

Enumerate: Write in list or outline form, presenting points concisely one by one.

Evaluate: Carefully appraise all the advantages and limitations you can think of. Try to balance authorities' views with your own.

Examine: Describe the material in close detail and include others' descriptions if possible.

Explain: Clarify and interpret the material you present. Account for differences of opinion or results, and say why they occur.

Illustrate: Demonstrate the point(s) with a figure, picture, diagram or practical example.

Interpret: Translate in your own words, with examples.

Justify: Prove (with evidence) or give reasons for decisions or conclusions; make sure you are convincing.

List: Similar to 'enumerate'; write an itemised series of concise statements.

Outline: Organise a description under main points and a few subordinate points, leaving out minor details. Just the general arrangement or classification of things is required here.

Prove: As for 'Justify': establish something by giving factual evidence, examples, or clear logical reasons.

Relate: Show how things are connected or similar to each other, or how one causes another.

Review: Examine a subject critically, analysing and commenting on its main points.

State: Present the main points in brief, clear sequence, with the minimum of details, illustrations or examples.

Summarise: Give the main points or facts in condensed form, leaving out details and illustrations.

Trace: Describe the progress, development or history of the subject, from its point of origin (unless some other starting-point is given).

Rule 2: List the questions you think the essay should answer

This gives you a framework for your essay and a focus for your research. A well-written piece can be built just like a house. The essay topic is the piece of land; the questions you ask yourself here, and which you will later answer, are the architect's plans. Think of each question as a label for a room in your house: for example, instead of a 'living room' it might be 'Where are the breeding sites?'. The number of 'rooms' in your 'house' depends on the length of the essay. For a long essay, ask more questions or else give more detailed answers to the questions you choose.

Rule 3: Research and make notes

Remember to keep to your topic and your outline, but don't be afraid to make changes if they are necessary. For example, suppose for your question about the breeding habits of fish you have difficulty finding information about the breeding sites but find really interesting facts about the way they protect their eggs. At the research stage you can change the question *as long as* it still fits into the general structure: you have to have a logical reason for putting a skating rink where you should have a bedroom.

Rule 4: Read all your notes and sort them into a logical order

One good way of dealing with this part of the process is to number your questions, read each note, decide which question it belongs with and number it accordingly. If a note applies to more than one section, put both numbers at the top of the page to remind you to indicate this. Then, check to see if any section needs more information. You may have to go back to the library for it, but if no more is available, other sections may have enough information to make up for this. Not every section will be exactly the same length as every other.

Rule 5: Write a draft. Then write another draft

Don't be precious about your work: it can almost always be improved on the second or third attempt. Even though I've been using a computer/word processor for the last 5 years I still write almost everything on paper the first time. It's easier to spread out sheets of paper on my desk, or the floor, or a large table, and pick the ones I need for each section.

Quite often I take the first draft and either draw lines, use asterisks and other signs to show the changed order of paragraphs, or cut the paper into sections and rearrange them. At first this seems tedious, but with a little practice it becomes habit and improves your output quite significantly.

Remember John, from Rule 1? He also wrote far more than he should have. It takes skill and discipline to stick to a word limit. When you write too much it is usually either irrelevant or waffly. In either case you need to cut back. Editing is also a skill, and one well worth developing. Learn to read your own work critically. Look for information that is nice but unnecessary and cut it out. I know that sometimes you feel as though you're cutting out your most elegantly written sentences, but with practice you'll be able to make the essay elegant by cutting out the waffle.

Rule 6: Proofread your final draft carefully

The spellcheck facility on a word processor only picks up typing errors or spelling errors: it doesn't pick up words that are wrong in other ways. For example, suppose you type 'you' instead of 'your'. Both are correct English words, even if you would never use one in the place of the other, so the machine lets it go. These mistakes can be picked up only by reading through your own work very carefully. Sometimes it is helpful if someone else reads your work: they see it with fresh eyes. You could, in exchange, read theirs.

Rule 7: Acknowledge your sources

Make sure that you reference your work according to the system used in your course—see Chapter 18 for an explanation of these technical parts of your essay. This is important if you want to avoid any suspicion of plagiarism. You must acknowledge all your information sources, even if they were all given as a reading list.

Those are my rules for writing essays. As you get some practice writing them you will probably change some of the rules and add others to suit your own particular style of working, and that's fine. As I have already said, be flexible, make things work for you. When you feel you've finished your first essay, use this checklist or the guide that follows it to mark it yourself, then compare this with the mark the teacher or lecturer gives you.

Checklist

1 Does the essay answer the question or deal with the topic that was set?
2 Does it cover all the main aspects and in sufficient depth?
3 Is the content accurate and relevant?
4 Is the material logically arranged?
5 Is each main point well supported by examples and argument?
6 Does it clearly distinguish your ideas from those of others?
7 Do you acknowledge all sources and references?
8 Is the length of the essay right for its purpose?
9 Is it written plainly and simply, without clumsy or obscure phrasing? (A good test is to read it out loud.)
10 Is the grammar, punctuation and spelling acceptable, and (if it's handwritten) is it legible?

Marking guide for essays

Use this guide to check that the structure of your essay is what it should be. Give your essay a tick in the margin for every one of the following features it contains. If your total is over 16, you should feel confident about handing it in for marking. If not, rewrite it. Put the tick right next to the item it applies to in the essay.

Introduction

- First sentence makes a general statement of your aims or case line, in your own words.
- Second sentence summarises the main points you make in the body of the essay, in the order they appear.

- Doesn't simply copy the question.
- Is less than 8 lines (use your discretion).

Main body

Score yourself as follows for each of the three best paragraphs that follow the introduction.

- Paragraph has a clear topic sentence (usually comes first).
- Presents evidence (examples, quotations, statistics, and so on).
- Gives some idea of how this paragraph relates to the question and how it helps to answer it.
- Last sentence contains a 'hook' that links that paragraph to the next one.

Conclusion

- Summarises the main statement concisely and clearly (without simply repeating it).
- Summarises the supporting arguments.
- Shows the reader how your essay has answered the question satisfactorily.
- Leaves the reader with a 'punchline'.

Reports

A report is a systematic, logical, attractively presented statement of facts, ideas, judgments—and sometimes recommendations—directed to a specific reader who needs this data to reach a sound decision. In the early stages of your studies you are more likely to be reading research reports than writing them. Knowing how to write them helps you to understand and assess the ones you read.

Like good essays, reports also have an introduction, a body and a conclusion. Some reports also have a section, after the body but before the conclusion, that recommends actions that should or shouldn't be taken as a result of the report's findings. Reports are usually drawn up from detailed research and can be fairly lengthy. An essay tends to show both sides of an argument, but a report usually provides information without opinion, except in the recommendations.

Knowing the ABC of report writing will help you to keep your reports:

Accurate

Brief

Clear

And remember, 'brief' doesn't necessarily mean a short essay here, but one that leaves out unnecessary detail. So let's look at how you plan and prepare a report.

First, be sure you understand the purpose of the report. Write this down in one sentence. It could be to provide information, to analyse facts, to put forward ideas or to recommend a course of action.

Next, think about who will read the report and why. What would the reader want to know? What does the reader already know? How will the reader use the report? Even if the report is for a class or tutorial assignment, the lecturer will probably have given you some background information. If not, ask the teacher to suggest sources.

Now it's time to start collecting all the facts and ideas related to the subject that you can find, and from as many sources as possible. You could use various techniques such as observations, interviews, discussions, surveys, questionnaires and investigations besides books and other publications. Take lots of notes, and don't forget to write down the source of your information. If you interview people be sure to make notes even if you use a tape recorder. Don't put all your eggs in one basket. Tape recorders do all sorts of strange things: batteries dry up, tapes become tangled and sometimes you even forget to press the 'record' button!

Questionnaires are handy when you want to collect data from a lot of people and don't have time to interview them. On the other hand, setting the questions is not always easy. They have to be very clear so they won't be misunderstood, and then you have to be careful about the conclusions you draw from the answers.

Library searches involve reading all kinds of books, journals, bulletins, articles, reports, etc. Again, be careful to collect all the information about the source (see Chapter 18) for your bibliography.

Visual aids such as diagrams, maps, photographs and charts should only be used if they clarify the content of the report. Unnecessary graphics make it too bulky and annoy the reader.

Principal parts of a report

Your report may have all of these parts, or, if it's a fairly short one, only some of them.

Title page

This identifies the report. It states the title, the author, the reader—and this can be something generic like 'Construction workers' or 'Mature-age students'—and the date of completion. The title of your report should be factual and informative—this isn't a mystery novel.

Letter of transmittal

Sometimes called a 'cover letter', this explains who requested the report and briefly summarises it. This could be attached to the cover page.

Table of contents

You'll need this if your report is more than 3 or 4 pages long. It shows the major and minor sections and outlines the structure. It should also contain a list of diagrams, charts, tables and so on.

Summary

Sometimes called a synopsis, it very briefly summarises the contents of the report. Add it to a long report so that people see whether it is worth reading the whole report.

Introduction

This tells the reader what your report contains. If it's well written and convincing people are more likely to read the rest. Here you should also give the reader an idea of the problems you found, your method of research, and the objectives of your study.

Body of the report

Obviously this is the largest part of your report and it should be logically ordered, easy to read, easy to understand and pleasing to look at. One way of presenting it well is to number the sections (or main headings), sub-headings and points. For example:

1. Sub-heading
   1.1 First point.
   1.2 Second point relating to the same sub-heading.

Each point may have more than one paragraph and in some reports each paragraph is numbered—1.1.1, 1.1.2, 1.1.3 and so on—but this is only necessary when the report is very long or if points are referred to in other documents.

Your sub-headings should be clear and lead your reader

logically through the information you are presenting and the conclusions you have drawn from it.

Recommendations

This gives the reader solutions and recommends courses of action to take (or avoid) concerning the information presented in the body of the report. If there is more than one possible solution or course of action, indicate which you prefer and explain why.

Conclusion

Here you summarise your report very briefly, noting the main points of the data and of your recommendations. At the end put your name, signature and the date.

Appendix

This is where you put any supplementary material that would interrupt the flow of the body of the report. It could include photographs, maps, charts, experiment results, a very recent update of material, or any other data that would clarify the report.

Bibliography

This is a list of your sources of information and Chapter 18 gives you detailed information on how to put this together.

Having done your research, written a draft and checked your facts, you are now ready to do the final draft. Here is a checklist to ensure that you haven't left anything out.

Checklist for report writing

Do you have all the necessary parts?

- Title page
- Table of contents
- Summary (or synopsis)
- Introduction
- Body of the report
- Recommendations (or discussion)
- Conclusion
- Appendix
- Bibliography

Have you checked your grammar, spelling and general flow of language? Does it make sense to you? If there is time, ask a friend to read it through and make comments.

Other writing

This chapter has covered the main forms of writing you will have to do during your studies. These assignments are what mature students worry the most about. Once you have a blueprint and you've written two or three, you'll wonder why you ever thought it would be so hard. But it takes practice and perseverance and you can practise by writing anything. Keeping a journal is a very good way of getting practice without having to show your writing to anyone else. Writing letters to the newspaper or your favourite magazine is another way of learning to say what you want in a clear, concise way. Try writing letters to a friend, or start with postcards if you don't think you'll find enough to say. You will have other writing assignments—instructions, definitions, directions—but compared to essays and reports they will seem really simple.

One last tip: start thinking about the structure of the things you read. Whether these are books, pamphlets, instructions for your newest appliance or a recipe, think about what has been written and whether you could write it more clearly. Most of all, enjoy what you do: it will show through in your work.

18

The fiddly bits

THE TITLE FOR THIS CHAPTER CAME FROM someone else—I can't remember who, but I completely understand how they feel. Many students find it difficult to remember to put in all the references they should, even though lecturers hand out information about plagiarism at the beginning of every course. The difference between plagiarism and cheating is that we think of cheating as something we do in tests and exams and plagiarism is a concept we don't hear about until we get into higher levels of study.

To avoid any suggestion of plagiarism you must note where you found every single piece of information you use in your written work.

Quotations and citations

A quotation is a passage or remark you have quoted directly from someone else's work. It must always appear in quotation marks and in the author's exact words. If you change, leave out or add any words you must make this clear with *square* brackets and ellipses, as follows:

'Our Father [and Mother] which art in Heaven . . .'

'Our [Parent] . . . in Heaven . . .'

When there seems to be some sort of error in the original publication, leave it as is and add '(sic)' like this:

'Daisy Ashford's novel *The Young Visiters* (sic)'.

A citation is the reference to another book, journal article or any other published work. When you don't use the exact words of the original author you must still show the source of your information. This serves two purposes: it prevents any suspicion of plagiarism and it ensures that you get credit for your own original ideas. Plagiarism means presenting another person's thoughts, writings, inventions and so on as your own. It isn't difficult to understand how this would upset people, and it can even escalate to legal troubles.

There are two widely used referencing systems—and several less well known. For good grades, it is absolutely vital to find out from the beginning what system your particular lecturer or teacher wants. It isn't enough to get the institute ruling because that is usually too general. In fact most of the style booklets I've seen tell you about both systems and then leave it to the faculty or even the lecturer to decide. In any case, make sure you get a style guide (sometimes called 'referencing procedures') from your university or college when you enrol. The two most common systems are known as 'traditional footnoting' and 'the Harvard system'. And remember: find out at the beginning of the course which one you should use.

Traditional footnoting

In one system the footnotes refer to bibliographical details—check the section in this chapter on bibliographies. Your writing will include numbers like this[1] to show that you are referring to someone else's work. At the bottom (foot) of the page that number appears again with the name of the author, the title of the book or article, the name of the journal or periodical and volume number if it's an article, the place of publication, the year of publication, and the number(s) of the page(s) where your citation appeared.

Footnotes are also used for additional, non-essential, information related to the matter being discussed. This system is used less often in short pieces of writing but quite often in books. It can be annoying to read, and, as George Bernard Shaw once said, if it's important it should be in the main text and if it's not it should be left out altogether.

The Harvard system

In this system you use the name of the author or authors, the year of publication and the page number at the point where you are referring to their work. For example:

> Memories are not chance happenings. We can 'tune our brain to think in a particular way' (O'Connor & Seymour, 1990, p.37) but we need 'triggers' (Lazear, 1990, p.5). We also need to decide whether we need the information for short or long term use (Marshall & Rowland, 1986, p.38) when we study.

The Harvard system does also allow for footnotes, but only the kind that explain something or add information. A good way to edit your footnotes is to decide whether they are really necessary. If the information is important the contents of the footnote can usually be included in the main body of the text. If it really doesn't seem to fit in it may not be necessary at all. When you use footnotes in the Harvard system you use a symbol such as an asterisk, and repeat this at the bottom of the page with the information.

All that sounds like a lot of work but it's really important. First of all because you don't want to be accused of plagiarism, secondly because it proves that you've done your reading.

Bibliographies

Having done all the right referencing in the body of your assignment or report, you need to list, in alphabetical order according to authors' surnames, all the books, journals, videos and so on from which you got your ideas and information. Just like so many other things in the education field, there are some fairly strict rules about how to put together a bibliography. When your source is a book, your bibliography entry will look like this:

Harris, K., *Teachers and Classes,* London, Routledge & Kegan Paul, 1982.

1 Name of author (or editor), surname first, followed by initials.
2 Title of the book, in italics or underlined if you cannot produce italics.
3 Volume number, if applicable.
4 Place of publication, name of publisher and year of publication, in that order.

When you use information from a journal article the bibliographic entry looks like this:

Gollan, P., 'Nationalism and Politics in Australia before 1851', *Australian Journal of Politics and History,* Vol. 1, No. 1, November 1955, pp. 33–48.

1 Author's name (as for books).
2 Title of the article in single inverted commas.
3 Name of journal, in italics (otherwise, underlined).

141

4 Series number (if applicable), volume number, date of issue and pages occupied by the article.

Video and audio sources

In the bibliography these sources are treated the same as other entries except that instead of an author or editor the producer's name is entered, and instead of a publisher you enter the production company. You also enter the year in which the production was made.

Interviews

If your research includes interviews with people who are experts in their field, you must enter them in your bibliography. Give their title, name and initial, their field of expertise, the name of their company, institution and so on (for example, 'Dr X. Pell, Investigating Officer, Rodent Division, CSIRO'), followed by the words 'private interview'. If possible, attach a transcript of the interview to your assignment—provided, of course, that it was reasonably short. You don't want to have to transcribe a 30-minute interview, but a 5-minute one shouldn't be too difficult.

19

Exams

IF YOU ARE LIKE MOST MATURE STUDENTS you'll probably read this chapter before you even enrol in any course. At school we were all afraid of exams; in some cases the teachers even went to the trouble to make sure that we were frightened. Some of us learned to cope with the feeling, but many of us didn't. Just the word is enough to bring on a nervous attack. So, let's look at what happens, how to cope and how to plan for the exams that still form a significant part of the assessment for most formal courses.

Preparing for the exam can be divided into three main parts:

1 long-term preparation
2 short-term preparation
3 before, during and after.

Looking at them one by one should help you to overcome most of the fear. Note, I didn't say all the fear. We need a little anxiety so that the adrenalin this produces can drive us through the event. Too much confidence, however, is almost as bad as paralysing fear.

Long-term preparation

This should start within the first week of classes. University courses give you information about exams when you enrol. TAFE colleges hand out assessment schedules within the first 2 weeks of classes. These tell you when assignments are due and when tests and exams will take place. At this point you don't need definite dates, but you do need to know how regular the assessment system will be, and what it consists of. Most require assignments to be handed in during the course and then an exam at the end. Check the weighting of each. If the assignments carry more than half the marks you may be better off concentrating on them. Getting good marks for the assignments was always easier for me than getting good marks in exams, where I got so nervous that my mind went blank and I sat there, hardly able to write. This went on until someone taught me some relaxation techniques and how to use them in stressful situations. Knowing exam dates helps you to plan your studies and avoid last-minute cramming, which only makes you feel more nervous. So, let's get back to our planning.

Take notes in class. Remember, use key words and concepts to make revision easier. Go back to Chapter 15 on note-taking. Keep together all your teacher handouts and other relevant topic list material to give you an idea of topics and assessment requirements for the exam. Also look at past exam papers in the library, speak to students who have done the course before and ask questions in class. Speak to students who had the same teacher and get tips about what hints the teacher gives—they all do!—during lessons about possible exam questions.

The next step is to make a weekly study timetable and stick to it. If something unexpected comes up and you really can't stick to your timetable, try to make up the time during the next week or two. Time, like the water in the river, never comes round twice. Try to become as familiar with the material as you can. This is why I feel that mature-age students should choose subjects they enjoy. When you enjoy something it isn't a chore, it becomes something you look forward to.

If you're having trouble planning your time, revise Chapter 5 for helpful hints on time management.

Short-term preparation

This should begin 2–3 weeks before the exam. Set aside some time each day especially for revision. Note that this is definitely not a time to be learning new material.

There is an art to revision which gives you confidence when you walk into the exam room. Cramming at the last minute is sure to make you more nervous. So how do you revise effectively? Here is my 5-point plan.

1   Read through all the material you have that is relevant to the topic you are revising. Don't add anything new at this stage—it's too late.
2   When you've finished reading—and this doesn't have to be in one sitting—put the work aside for at least an hour or two, and not more than a day or two. When you're ready to go on, get a large sheet of paper for each separate topic area.
3   On the first sheet, write the name of one topic area inside a circle in the middle of the page. Now, write down everything you can remember about the topic. Link things that relate to one another with lines, arrows or whatever. Use coloured pencils if this helps you. Group things to jog your memory. This is a mind-map. It is the only way I know to show me what I don't know.
4   When you've put as much as you can on the mind-map go back to your notes and study materials and compare them, marking anything in the notes that your map

doesn't have. These are the points you now have to revise more carefully. Anything you put on the map has been lodged in your long-term memory: if you could put it on your mind-map, you will be able to recall it during the exam. The only thing that may hinder you in the exam is nerves. The other advantage of the map is that during the 'reading time' at the beginning of the exam you will be able to replicate it.

5   Revise any material you didn't put on the map and then repeat steps 3 to 5.

Another way to revise your work is to explain it to a friend. Tell them the main points of various concepts in your course. By doing this without written notes, you fix the concept more clearly in your mind. Studying with a friend can also give you some fresh insights into the subject. Writing summaries of the material you need to learn is also helpful. More than that, it is good practice for writing answers in the exam.

During this short-term preparation stage it's also helpful to practise with previous exam papers. Time yourself to see if you can write enough in the time normally allowed for that exam.

Before . . .

On the day before the exam, take it easy. Don't study too hard or try to learn anything new. Go through your summaries, have another look at your mind-maps. Check some of the questions that have come up on other papers and think about how you would answer them. Don't study late into the night, but try to get a good night's sleep.

On the exam day itself try not to rush. Give yourself enough time to find the room, especially if you haven't been there before. I did all my exams for New England University in the overwhelming atmosphere of Sydney

University. It added to my terror that I never seemed to have time to find out in advance where to go. If you have time, read through some of your summaries, or notes, just to reassure yourself.

Don't talk to anyone who may worry you about the exam. This is the time when you need positive self-talk, not any negative input from anyone else.

During . . .

When you walk into the room, find your seat and sit down. Arrange on the desk your pens, pencils, ruler, sharpener, lollies, drink bottle and whatever else you need. Unless you have X-ray vision don't try to guess what's on the upside-down question paper.

Sit straight in the chair, put your hands in your lap or on the desk and make a conscious effort to relax them. When your hands are completely relaxed take a deep breath and let it out slowly, relaxing your body as you do. Repeat this several times, then open your eyes. Unless you were very early it will be time to turn the paper over—but wait until you're told to or you may find yourself disqualified.

Once you've turned the paper over skim right through quickly, then read it again carefully. Mark the questions that score most. Also mark the questions you will find easiest to answer. Do these first because you can get them out of the way fairly quickly. This gives you a start, like warming up an engine. Once you get going, it becomes easier to keep going, so be sure to do all the questions that carry the most marks, starting with the easiest.

Most exams have a reading time at the beginning—usually about 10 minutes—during which you can make notes on some rough paper or on the question paper but not in the answer book. Use this time to build small mind-maps or lists of points about each question. Put down only as much as you can think of easily. Don't agonise over any question if you think you don't have enough information. Go on to the next one and you will probably remember things a few minutes later. Our subconscious minds are wonderful.

As you go through the questions making notes, also allocate a certain amount of time to each question. When you start writing try to stick to these times. For example, suppose the exam time is 3 hours, and there are 20 questions to answer. Three questions require long answers and the others all need short (but not one or two word) answers. Allow 20 minutes for each of the long answers—60 minutes—and about 5 minutes each for the short answers—about 90 minutes: a total of 2½ hours. This, if you achieve the goal, will give you about 30 minutes to go through your work, checking your spelling, grammar and handwriting, all of which can suffer when we are writing under stress.

Once you start writing, keep an eye on the clock. Pace yourself, don't go too fast but try to keep to the times you allocated to each answer. If you run out of time use point form to answer the last few questions. Just don't panic. You can only do your best.

If, during the exam, you have a 'mental block' don't panic. Leave a space and go on to the next question. Tell yourself that you'll remember it in a while and keep writing. After a while the information probably will come to you in a flash when you least expect it. Of course, this blinding flash might happen when you're having coffee with someone hours after the exam is over, but during the exam don't let a mental block stop you from completing the other questions.

And after . . .

Don't discuss the exam with any of the other students immediately after writing. This can be nerve-racking and will do you absolutely no good if you have another exam soon after. The best thing you can do is to put the exam out of your mind. Look at it this way: you did your best at the time; you can't change even one small fullstop on the paper after you've handed it in; and the worst thing that can happen is that you fail the exam. The world won't end. You won't die. You may be a bit embarrassed if your family expected you to pass. You'll certainly feel disappointed. With luck there will have been assessment tasks through the semester and you'll have passed those well enough to give you a pass average. Until I learned to cope with exams by using the tips I've given I got through on the strength of the marks I got for assignments.

So hang in there: you too will learn to live through exams, but it does take a conscious effort for most of us.

Afterword

 IT DOESN'T MATTER WHERE YOU ARE ON THE education scale, whether you're doing pottery at a local adult education centre or a PhD at a top university, it should be enjoyable. Life wasn't meant to be easy, but it wasn't meant to be boring or stressful either.

And remember, with all the other demands on your time your studies may sometimes have to be put on hold. When this happens don't let the door slam behind you. Talk to teachers, coordinators, counsellors, anyone who can help to ensure that when you are ready to come back you won't have to start all over again. Put all the paperwork you collected in a safe place and try to keep up your reading, no matter how little, until you can get back.

Most of all be aware that learning is really a lifelong process, not just a short course you do for the first 10–12 years of your life. So, hang in there: it really gets better and better.

Further reading

This is a short selection of books that I found helpful at various stages of my own studies. Any library will certainly have a selection of other books on any of these subjects and I would suggest that you browse through the catalogue and check some of them: you never know when you'll find something useful.

Part 1: The student in you

Honey, P. and Mumford, A., *The Manual of Learning Styles*, England, P. Honey, 1980

Marshall, L.A. and Rowland, F., *A Guide to Learning Independently*, Melbourne, Longman Cheshire, 1986

Smith, M.J., *When I Say No, I Feel Guilty*, New York, Bantam Books, 1981

Part 2: Setting yourself up for study

Brem, C., *Are We on the Same Team Here?*, Sydney, Allen & Unwin, 1995

Orr, F., *How to Succeed at Part-Time Study*, Sydney, Allen & Unwin, 1988

Part 3: Getting the most out of your study

Lazear, D., *Seven Ways of Knowing*, Australia, Hawker Brownlow Education, 1991

O'Connor, J. and Seymour, J., *Introducing Neuro-Linguistic Programming*, London, Harper Collins, 1990

Part 4: Showing what you've learned

Anderson, J., Durston, B.H. and Poole, M., *Thesis and Assignment Writing*, Sydney, Wiley, 1984

Orr, F., *How to Pass Exams*, Sydney, Allen & Unwin, 1984

Strunk, W. Jr and White, E.B., *The Elements of Style*, London, Macmillan, 1972

Turabian, K.L., *A Manual for Writers*, Chicago, Chicago University Press, 1973